Time For Leadership

The Accomplishing More in Less Time, Less Effort, and Less Stress Leadership Program Guide

Pierre Khawand

ISBN: 978-1492135838

ACKNOWLEDGEMENTS

Special thanks to the People-OnTheGo faculty members who contributed their knowledge and expertise to our leadership program and to the corresponding chapters in this book. Daniel Guillory, CEO of Innovations International, discusses the imperative topic of creativity and innovation in Chapter 8. Dr. Alicia Ruelaz Maher takes stress management to a whole new level in her discussion in Chapter 9. Deanna Moncrief, Principal of Benchmark Wellness, explores key principles in Chapter 10 that bring nutrition and wellness within reach. Jennifer Weland, Principal of Evolve Fitness & Coaching, covers the fundamentals of movement and exercise in Chapter 11, explaining how to overcome obstacles and engage into rewarding physical exercises of all kinds.

Big thanks to longtime supporter Steve Loosley for his encouragement during this effort, his review of the chapters, his comments and suggestions, and valued business insights. I also would like to thank the People-OnTheGo Online Community Manager, Melissa Sweat, for her help in making the leadership program a success, Verona Tanihara for her help with editing and revising the manuscript, and Jenny Seiler for her contribution to the visual graphics.

I also would like to thank the leadership survey participants who took the time to answer the leadership survey and contributed to this effort, and Adrian Ott, CEO of Exponential Edge and author of *The 24-Hour Customer*, for partnering with me and bringing her leadership insights into the survey findings and report.

Last but not least, thanks to my family and friends, whose support and engagement have been most instrumental to the completion of this yet another exciting journey.

I hope you enjoy reading *Time for Leadership* and take these behaviors to your work and personal life to create accomplishments and happiness for you, your team, your organization, and your community!

Table of Contents

Welcome Letter, by Pierre Khawand

Welcome to a whole new world of leadership. Leadership demystified. Leadership broken down into digestible and practical behaviors. Leadership upgraded for the 21st century and made attainable for everyone who wants it. I invite you to join me in this journey, making your world and the world around you more fulfilling, as well as creating amazing results for you, your team, your organization, and your community.

Our leadership survey participants and leadership program participants concurred that effective leadership needs to include the following: focusing on results, setting expectations, the ability to negotiate, motivating teams, managing conflicts, time management, stress management, organization, taking initiative, technology savvy, social media savvy, having compassion, awareness of self, awareness of others, creativity, and innovation. The three that ranked the highest were awareness of self, awareness of others, and motivating teams. This reflects the dire need for increased awareness all around.

The journey you are about to undertake is primarily a journey of awareness. Not awareness for the sake of awareness, however, but awareness translated to actionable behaviors and, therefore, tangible results and happier lives.

The leadership concepts and behaviors presented in this book are ideal for functional managers and team leaders who want to create results and develop people, as well as senior managers who want to change culture and take their organizations to the next level. Note, however, that we are experiencing an important paradigm shift when it comes to leadership. Leadership is no longer seen as reserved for the select few who are in charge. While everyone agrees that it is imperative for managers and supervisors to develop leadership skills, 67 percent of the survey participants indicated that front line employees need leadership skills as well, and 63 percent indicated that individual contributors need them, too. Who wouldn't benefit from increased awareness of self and awareness of others, after all? How about the ability to set expectations and negotiate, as well as take initiative?

One more paradigm shift relates to the valuable lessons that the well-known dance the tango can teach us about productivity and leadership—not only that it takes two to tango, which translates into engagement and collaboration, but also that the line between following and leading is no longer as strictly defined as it may have been in the past. Just like on the dance floor, leaders need to let go of leading at times and allow followers to respond and take initiative. Followers need to seize opportunities to initiate and lead.

Join us to learn and appreciate this dynamic approach to leadership. Your key takeaways will be:

- Strategies, tools, and behaviors for staying focused on the desired results and leading others effectively in today's complex and diverse work environment

- Awareness of one's own personality and leadership style and the styles of others, in order to increase personal and professional effectiveness and enhance collaboration and teamwork

- Practical methods for managing stress, mastering nutrition, and using physical exercise to rejuvenate and achieve optimum performance

I also invite you to become part of our learning community, which includes thousands of professionals who want to be more effective and more fulfilled at work and beyond, as well as contribute more fully to their organizations and to their communities. Here are ways in which you can become part of this community:

- Join the "Accomplishing more with less group" on Facebook

- Join the "Accomplishing more with less group" on LinkedIn

- Connect with me on Twitter (@pierrekhawand)

- Join our complimentary lunch & learn webinars at:
  www.people-onthego.com/free-webinars

- Check out our leadership program and workshops at:
  www.people-onthego.com/workshops

Chapter 1: Your Leadership Journey Starts Here

A journey of a thousand miles begins with a single step!

Congratulations for taking the first step in this imperative journey. Let us get going. It is time for leadership. This means the time has come for you to tackle leadership and embark on this fulfilling challenge. Today's work environment necessitates leadership at all levels. It is about time we realize that leadership is not just for the so-called leaders. Instead, its reach needs to be broadened to all levels within each organization. Time for leadership also means making time for leading. Leaders who don't have time aren't leading. Time for leadership is an awakening in modern leadership.

In the time for leadership era, speed matters. This is a fundamental concept that I will continue to develop in this journey. This may appear to be simplistic. It is not. It is revolutionary when you consider the five dimensions of speed that I tackle. First comes physical speed. This means bodily moving faster from point A to point B, whatever the context is. This is the most basic and most obvious element of speed. It does have merits, but in the world of knowledge work, it is less significant than the next dimension, which is mental speed. Mental speed is where breakthroughs start to happen. Mental speed is about staying focused. It is retraining our brain to be more focused and less scattered. It is more than just focus, however. It is also about working in bursts. Bursts of focused time, followed by bursts of collaborative time, and then bursts of playtime! This is a breakthrough model that I will introduce later. Following these first two concepts of speed come strategic speed, emotional speed, and psychological speed. All together, these five dimensions will result in quantum leaps in your ability to tackle leadership and create amazing results.

Like any meaningful journey, time for leadership starts by creating a vision for what we want to accomplish. You're invited to reflect on this vision and formulate specific goals. These goals enable you to apply the leadership behaviors in the real world and gain valuable experience. Without behaviors and real-world experience, leadership remains theoretical and elusive. The goals include a leadership-related project, a work-related project that you want to complete successfully, a strengths development plan, a wellness goal, and a personal goal. These five goals give your journey meaning and passion. Don't just read through them; buckle down and start envisioning.

A leadership project

Envision a new project or initiative that will enable you to practice and demonstrate leadership behaviors ranging from taking initiative to working with a variety of stakeholders, as well as inspiring and motivating people, negotiating and managing resources, solving problems and making decisions, and, most importantly, leading to a successful completion. A leadership project may consist of a process improvement, a business case or business plan for a new product or service, a marketing or sales plan, or any such innovative and bold initiative that challenges you and leads to growth and accomplishment.

A work project

Identify a work-related project in which you can also practice and demonstrate leadership. While the leadership project is supposed to be visionary and ambitious, the work-related project is more tangible and concrete, based on the routine work that you currently do. Your goal is to turn this project into a learning opportunity and lead it like never before. The work-related project is where the rubber hits the road. Leadership is wishful thinking until you use it in your daily endeavors and until the people around you notice the change and feel motivated and supported yet accountable. It is also wishful thinking until you create significant value for your stakeholder. If your work projects tend to be long-term undertakings, make this leadership project an important milestone within the long term project, so you can complete it within the next few weeks or months.

Your Strengths Development Plan

In preparation for this plan, I urge you to take the StrengthsFinder assessment:

https://www.gallupstrengthscenter.com/Purchase/

Purchase the Strengths Discovery Package ($9.99). It will only take about thirty-five minutes to complete the assessment, and the information that you glean will be transformational. Download your Signature Themes Report, the Strengths Insight and Action-Planning Guide, and the Strengths Insight Guide.

There are nine items that I suggest you include in your Strengths Development Plan. The first five items have to do with your top five strengths, as identified in the StrengthsFinder and referred to as Your Signature Themes. Review your Strengths Insight and Action-Planning Guide, particularly Section II ("Application"). For each of your top five strengths, identify one action from the list of suggested actions that you can take repeatedly to enhance and better leverage that strength.

While it is tempting to select multiple actions for each of your strengths, for now, please choose only one action per strength. Feel free to tailor the action that you choose in order to make it more meaningful and appropriate to your needs. (See item 4 in the table below as an example of a tailored action.)

This is an example of what the first five items of a Strengths Development Plan might look like for someone whose top strengths are Achiever, Analytical, Focus, Learner, and Competition:

1	Achiever	Remember to build celebration and recognition.
2	Analytical	Find the best way of expressing my thoughts, so I can help and support others on my team.
3	Focus	Others are likely to think, act, and talk less efficiently than I do. Instead of being annoyed by their "detours," pay attention to potential discoveries and delights.
4	Learner	Attend the upcoming project management conference. Present key observations and trends to my team.
5	Competition	When I win, I want to take the time to investigate why I won and use this as a learning opportunity for me and to share with others.

The sixth, seventh, and eighth items in your Strengths Development Plan relate to additional strengths that are unique to you. While the StrengthsFinder helped you identify some of your natural abilities, now it is time for you to dig deeper into the more specific, specialized experiences and accomplishments that you have had.

For instance, you may have in-depth experience in the Agile software development process or developed thorough knowledge of Customer Relationship Management (CRM) enterprise systems or been the liaison between end users and engineers. You may have presented to and communicated effectively with a board of directors or successfully managed and motivated project teams or attracted and recruited top talent in your field. There are many possibilities.

Select three such strengths, and for each one, identify an action that can help you further develop and leverage this strength. Here are some examples:

6	CRM systems	Become a guest blogger at some of the main blogs relating to the use of CRM systems.
7	Project Management	Share project management tips with my colleagues, and coach them on solving their project management challenges.
8	Explaining difficult concepts in simple terms	Schedule lunch & learn presentations to explain our technologies to our marketing and sales team.

Finally, the ninth item relates to a professional growth area that you want to develop further. This can be an interpersonal skill, a technical skill, an organizational skill, or it can be specific knowledge that you would like to acquire. Here are a few examples:

- Providing constructive feedback to my direct reports

- Delivering compelling presentations to customers

- Acquiring in-depth understanding of latest trends in Search-Engine-Optimization

- Becoming an effective public speaker

- Handling conflicts effectively

- Business writing

Item 9 may be as follows:

9	Public Speaking	Find opportunities to present to various groups, starting with informal presentations to internal groups and leading to presentations at industry conferences.

The resulting Strengths Development Plan would be:

1	Achiever	Remember to build celebration and recognition.
2	Analytical	Find the best way of expressing my thoughts, so I can help and support others on my team.
3	Focus	Others are likely to think, act, and talk less efficiently than I do. Instead of being annoyed by their "detours," pay attention to potential discoveries and delights.
4	Learner	Attend the upcoming project management conference. Present key observations and trends to the team.
5	Competition	When I win, I want to take the time to investigate why I won and use this as a learning opportunity for me and to share with others.
6	CRM applications	Become a guest blogger at some of the main blogs relating to the use of CRM applications.
7	Project Management	Share project management tips with my colleagues, and coach them on solving their project management challenges.
8	Explaining difficult	Schedule lunch & learn presentations to explain our technologies to our

	concepts in simple terms	marketing and sales team.
9	Public Speaking	Find opportunities to present to various groups, starting with informal presentations to internal groups and leading to presentations at industry conferences.

Once you have put your plan together, review the mix of items that you included, and look for synergies. Try to find actions that intersect multiple strengths and are therefore likely to produce bigger outcomes. For instance, if project management is one of the strengths that you would like to leverage (item 7 above), you happen to be a strong learner (item 4 above), and public speaking is one of the strengths that you want to develop (item 9 above), then the action "Attend the upcoming project management conference and present key observations and trends to the team" is a highly synergetic and effective one, because it covers all these strengths and developmental areas at once.

While implementing the Strengths Development Plan may seem to be a lot of work, it is actually less work than what it appears to be. You already have these strengths or at least have a good head start in most of these areas. The goal is to become more aware of these strengths and apply them more often. Knowing that these are your "strengths," applying them is easy and energizing.

A wellness-related goal

Identify one specific wellness-related goal in one of the following areas: exercise, nutrition, or stress management. Examples of these goals are as follows: run a marathon; lose twenty pounds; get cholesterol or glucose level to a desired range; reduce coffee, sugar, or alcohol intake to a certain level; etc. Select only one goal. You can always work on additional wellness areas later if you would like. However, in terms of your leadership program goals, it is important to identify one specific goal.

A personal goal

Identify a personal goal that would help you be happier and more fulfilled. This can relate to a personal relationship, being more involved in your community, taking on a new hobby, developing yet another skill, or overcoming a personal challenge of some sort. Some examples are as follows: improve my relationship with my partner; become more engaged in my daughter's activities in school; volunteer at a charitable organization; overcome my procrastination; and so on.

With the above five goals in hand, you are ready to embark on your leadership journey one behavior at a time! Chapter 2 introduces leadership behaviors. Leadership is wishful thinking unless we translate it into leadership behaviors.

Chapter 2: Managing Immediate Priorities and Long-Term Results

Your leadership journey is about one thing: Practicing leadership behaviors!

I do leadership, therefore I am a leader

These two words—leadership behaviors—say a lot about leadership!

First, they imply that leadership is not a mystery. It can be broken down to specific behaviors that you can learn and practice. What a relief! Second, they indicate that leadership is not something that you either have or you don't. It is something that you can mostly learn, building on the strengths that you already have. Another relief! Third, that leadership is not for the select few. It is for everyone who is willing to learn and practice at all levels within an organization. Leadership behaviors are powerful tools that can be utilized in both professional and personal life.

So, if you understand and practice the leadership behaviors, you will get more accomplished, and you will be happier, and so will your team and your organization. So will people at your home and in your community.

There are many behaviors that I will discuss and that you are invited to practice. Not just invited, but urged and implored to practice. Otherwise, leadership remains wishful thinking. These behaviors mostly fall within the following categories:

- Taking initiatives
- Focusing on results
- Developing people
- Thinking strategically
- Learning indefinitely

There are two secrets—or magic formulas, as I like to call them—that can make these types of behaviors exceptionally effective.

Secret #1: Behaviors work best in combinations

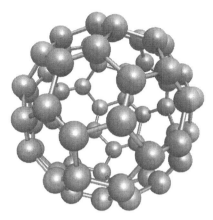

John Zenger and Joseph Folkman, in their book, *The Extraordinary Leader*[1], point out that in one of their surveys, they found that for leaders who ranked high on "focus on results" but not on "interpersonal skills," only 13 percent of them ranked high in their overall leadership effectiveness. And for those who ranked high on "interpersonal skills" but not on "focus on results," only 9 percent of them ranked high in their overall leadership effectiveness. Now here is the epiphany: For those who ranked high on both (focus on results and on interpersonal skills), 66 percent of them were ranked high in their overall leadership effectiveness.

The leadership behaviors build on each other. The total is greater than the sum. Hold on to your seat as you take this journey!

---

[1] John Zenger and Joseph Folkman, *The Extraordinary Leader: Turning Good Managers Into Great Leaders* (McGraw-Hill, 2009)

Secret #2: Behaviors help us rewire our brain

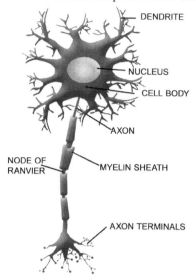

The second secret, or magic formula, has to do with neuroscience and how our brain works. With behaviors come certain thoughts and emotions, and we are likely to experience some *aha moments*. Dr. Alicia Maher, in her stress management work, describes an aha moment as consisting of a new branch forming in our brain between the neurons. If we continue to reinforce such a new branch, it will become stronger and overshadow old and ineffective branches. Over time, old branches fade away. This is referred to as neuroplasticity, which means our brain can change. Yes, we can rewire our brain, and that is what you will be doing as your practice these behaviors.

A simple behavior: What do I intend to accomplish today?

Let us start each day with a simple leadership behavior: Stopping and taking a moment to ask the question, "What do I want to accomplish today?"

This is not about diving into your e-mail, your to-do list, and your calendar in order to answer this question. It is about taking a minute or two to reflect on what is important and what you want to see accomplished at the end of the day. The result is a short list of strategic items that are going to make a difference. Having them in writing is likely to help you stay focused on results throughout the day.

Leadership starts here: The Immediate Priorities Matrix

If you are bombarded by competing priorities and feeling out of control or even overwhelmed, it is going to be challenging to practice leadership behaviors, let alone lead initiatives, projects, and people. That is why leadership starts with having such priorities well under control; hence, the AMLP[2] Immediate Priorities Matrix. Preparing the matrix is yet another simple behavior that can turn chaos into order.

The matrix includes a list of your short-term priorities in the left column, and in the next column, a breakdown of each priority into smaller steps. The right columns have the estimated time to implement the steps and the deadline or target completion date. What I didn't mention is the middle column. The middle column is the most important column in the matrix, and it identifies the "immediate" steps that are necessary to move this priority forward.

Priorities	Breakdown	Immediate	Time	Deadline

The scope of this matrix is short term. It is one or two weeks. It is intended to bring this information to one place and to the forefront. When this information is floating in our head, it can get overwhelming. When we see it in this simple format and turn it into "data" with specific steps, durations, and deadlines, it becomes digestible and actionable. The three actions are scheduling, setting expectations, and negotiating. This brings us back to leadership behaviors. Scheduling, setting expectations, and negotiating are three of the fundamental behaviors.

---

[2] AMLP refers to the Accomplishing More Leadership Program
http://www.people-onthego.com/accomplishing-more-leadership-program

Speed matters. In the information overload era, speed matters even more. Later in the book, I will discuss the five dimensions of speed. For now, I will simply note that preparing the matrix is intended to be a quick exercise. It is minutes and not hours. It is not about reproducing all the information you already have in project documents and elsewhere. It is about bringing your priorities quickly and succinctly into one place, and then bringing those priorities to the calendar so you can easily "see" them and "act" on them. The calendar is the only visual representation of time. The calendar is also a shared resource so others know how committed your time is.

However, be realistic with your scheduling. Leaders don't over-schedule. Remember that you need time to lead and time to handle the unexpected and the unknown. Schedule no more than 50 percent of your time.

The Immediate Priorities Matrix is the ultimate communication tool. In addition to bringing the next week or two into focus and releasing the stress that is associated with not knowing what's ahead, it also facilitates communication and problem solving. With your stakeholders, it provides you with the data you need to strengthen your position in negotiating convincing solutions to resource conflicts. With your team, instead of having ad-hoc and unfulfilling conversations about work loads and leaving your team stranded in the midst of confusing random demands, it enables you to coach your team members and help them work through such conflicting priorities. Use the matrix to turn an overwhelmed and dissatisfied team member into a motivated and energized ally.

Leadership ends here; focus on results

Enough with the two-week priorities! Let us take a look at the next three months and what you intend to accomplish in that time. In fact, you can only direct your vision toward the next three months if you have the next week or two well under control. Therefore the Immediate Priorities Matrix paved the road for what I am about to introduce, which is the AMLP End Results Matrix.

The End Results Matrix is intended to help you identify the key results that you want to accomplish in the next three months and, most importantly, how you're going to get there. This means reflecting on the initiatives, projects, and activities that are needed to get the results:

Result	Initiatives/Projects	Breakdown

It is imperative that results include personal and professional development elements.

Let us not stop with the matrix. It is all wishful thinking until you take action. This also means scheduling, setting expectations, and negotiating. Scheduling is different when it comes to the End Results Matrix. The activities here are all futuristic, and therefore you don't yet have the same level of specificity that you have in the Immediate Priorities Matrix. You might, for instance, schedule a working session with the appropriate resources two weeks from now in order to discuss and detail a certain activity. In parallel, you start to have formal and hallway conversations with the stakeholders to get buy-in and create excitement about these activities.

Leadership needs to end in results. No results, no leadership! The End Results Matrix is the vehicle.

The End Results Matrix for your leadership goals

In chapter 1, I discussed the leadership goals. It is time to turn these into an End Results Matrix and therefore into action. The matrix prompts you to reflect on and formulate how you are going to achieve these goals. This work of turning the goals into a matrix is tedious. It is very challenging, and it is likely that your avoidance and procrastination will kick in and slow you down or bring this process to a halt altogether. But fear not!

Fear not, because I have the antidote for avoidance and procrastination: Work in iterations and use a timer. Set your timer for thirty minutes and take a first stab at creating an initial outline. This is the first iteration. Then take a break or even put your matrix aside for a day or two before you approach the second iteration, which might be another thirty minutes of detailing your initial outline. The next iteration might focus on one of the goals, with the intention of completing the related section in the matrix. You get the point. Within days, you are likely to have your matrix and have conquered one of the most major obstacles in front of your leadership potential: avoidance and procrastination.

Your work goal, for instance, might be to complete the implementation of a new e-commerce site. This goal belongs in the first column of the matrix. Upon reflecting on this goal, you identify several activities that you need to undertake to accomplish it, including:

- Meet with the key players and establish rapport with them.

- Understand the current status and budget.

- Agree on the project objectives with the executive team.

- Communicate new project parameters to the team, and schedule key milestones.

- Establish weekly reports to monitor key milestones.

These activities belong in the second column of the matrix. In the third column, you translate each of the above activities into specific actions. "Meet with the key players and establish rapport with them" may translate into booking your flight, planning your agenda, and getting in touch with Joan to design a team-building session. After that comes scheduling, such as blocking thirty minutes on your calendar to book your flight, putting together an initial outline for the agenda and sending it to your team for feedback, and calling Joan to brief her about your needs.

If you are strong in the "Achiever" or "Arranger" areas in the StrengthsFinder assessment, creating matrices and scheduling is relatively easy for you. It is right up your alley. If these are not your strengths however, this work may present an enormous and potentially overwhelming challenge for you. In addition to working in iterations and using the timer, you might partner with someone on your team who has these strengths or perhaps find a coach, mentor, or friend who can help. The same applies when you have a team member who is struggling with turning their goals into actionable items. Help them do so or find someone who has these strengths to partner with them.

This highlights an important leadership behavior, which is leveraging strengths across your team and your organizations. If you practice appreciating and leveraging strengths, instead of focusing on weaknesses and trying to fix people's shortcomings, people feel motivated, confident, and paradoxically able to grow and overcome their weaknesses.

The matrix presents you with ample opportunities to practice the various types of leadership behaviors that I introduced earlier: taking initiative, focusing on results, developing people, thinking strategically, and learning indefinitely. As you practice, you engage your emotions and get these neurons to connect. You're then on your way to rewiring your brain the way you want it.

As I conclude this discussion of the End Results Matrix, one last thing to consider is whether you are setting ambitious goals that are exciting and challenging or whether you are settling for the ordinary and safe bets. If you want breakthroughs, you're invited to set the bar high. This is a form of leadership.

Leadership lives here: Better managing interruptions

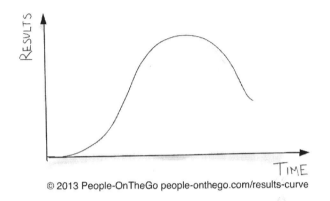

© 2013 People-OnTheGo people-onthego.com/results-curve

Let me show you how your results change with time when you are working on a task. If you are oblivious to this concept, your ability to lead is threatened. In my experience working with leaders at all levels, many leaders, who are otherwise capable and creative, seem to miss this concept and therefore sacrifice their ability to focus on results and their overall leadership effectiveness.

As shown in the chart above, when you start to work on a task, you start to get results, and as you continue, you get more results. At some point, however, the results level off and then diminish because you get mentally tired and are no longer productive, or you need someone else to do their part before you can continue, or you complete the task.

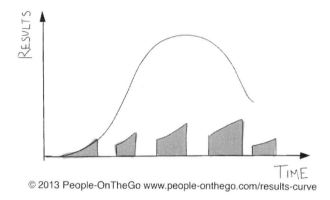

© 2013 People-OnTheGo www.people-onthego.com/results-curve

This is all good in theory, but what happens in reality is that a few minutes after you start to work on a task, you are interrupted (e-mail, phone, someone stops by, etc.). When you are interrupted, your results go down to zero. A few minutes later, you start again, and you start to make progress, but you get interrupted again. This time it's a chat message, your boss calling, or one of your team members has a question. Your results go down to zero again, and this happens repeatedly, as illustrated in the graph above. This is life in today's work environment.

This pattern is devastating for your overall results. Working this way, you get only a small fraction, maybe 5 to 10 percent, of the potential results that you would get if you were to stay focused. In addition, when you are working a few minutes here and a few minutes there, you are staying at a superficial level and not going deep into any particular project or line of thought.

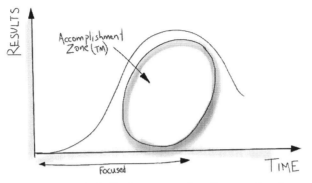

The point is that you need to stay on a task long enough to achieve the focused, in-depth thinking and creative problem solving that get meaningful things accomplished. This can take fifteen minutes, thirty minutes, or several hours, depending on the task. Once you have accomplished something worthwhile, it is time to stop your focused session and switch to being collaborative—to handle e-mail, make phone calls, and have live discussions. This is the work where you get most of your team's productivity and equally important results:

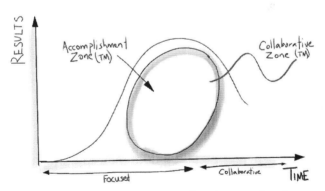

24

After the collaborative session, it is time to take a break—move, snack, recreate—do something that gets you re-energized and ready for the next focused session.

Working in Bursts

As I illustrated above, the best results are accomplished by working in bursts: alternating between bursts of focused effort, bursts of collaborative effort, and bursts of playtime. Each burst needs to be supported by the appropriate physical location, tools, and people. Leaders need to think carefully about how to enable themselves and their teams to work in bursts and support their team members in this endeavor.

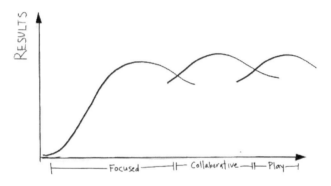

The focused burst (you can call it the "alone" burst) is likely to require silence and uninterrupted work, allowing you to dive deeply into the task at hand and unleash your creativity. Your surroundings need to be conducive to focus and ingenuity. Most offices aren't necessarily designed to support this burst, nor are the people at the office trained to behave in ways that support these bursts. Educating, enabling, and allowing your team to find the appropriate location, access the necessary tools, and get the support they need is imperative in today's climate of constant interruptions.

The collaborative burst requires access to the people with whom you want to collaborate, as well as the collaboration tools that can support this effort. If your team is in one office, then the office is

25

likely to be the ideal place for this burst. But if your team is spread among multiple offices and, perhaps, even time zones, then the physical location becomes less relevant, and access to effective collaboration tools becomes crucial.

While the play burst seems secondary, it is actually critical for productivity and engagement. This burst needs to happen whatever the location, and it needs to happen often. While many such bursts can be short periods of as little as a few minutes, more significant play bursts—and play-together bursts—are also vital to productivity.

While a play burst seems to imply an all-encompassing high-energy activity, it can actually be a short and simple exercise such as breathing[3], stretching, walking, or listening to your favorite music for a few minutes. Try this, for instance: Sit comfortably in your chair right now, close your eyes, and take a deep breath. Hold it for a few seconds and then exhale slowly and all the way. Take another deep, slow breath, and while doing so, straighten your back, relax your shoulders, and lift your chin a bit. Continue to breathe slowly in and out as you make these adjustments. You can add some meditational aspect by noticing any thoughts that come to your mind, imagining yourself jotting down each thought on a Post-it note, letting go of it, and seeing it fly in the air and slowly disappear into the skies. Continue to breathe slowly. Three minutes of this can have an amazing impact. The majority of our participants report an immediate change in how they feel in just three minutes. You are always only three minutes away from feeling better!

---

[3] Breathing exercise from our Stress Management class by Dr. Alicia Ruelaz Maher

The leader's day, from start to finish

As mentioned earlier, a leader's day starts with a moment of reflection, identifying what the leader intends to accomplish that day. The leader's day ends with a moment of reflection on what was accomplished, what lessons were learned, and what still needs to be accounted for and reconciled.

Moments of reflection are the necessary responses to information overload. Stopping the overload starts by stopping—stopping the trying to get things done and, instead, reflecting, in order to resume differently. What is keeping you busy is likely to be keeping you away from your amazing accomplishments. "No problem can be solved from the same level of consciousness that created it," said Albert Einstein. It is time to make space for reflection and discovery.

As you reflect on your intended accomplishments for the day, jot down these intentions in a journal. This helps to solidify your intentions and keep you on track throughout the day. Keep your journal handy at all times. It can serve as the extension of your short-term memory, allowing you to capture thoughts and events easily and quickly, instead of keeping them in your head buzzing around like busy bees. The journal also provides space for strategizing and for visual thinking. Dare to draw the issues and problems and relationships, to engage your whole brain and come up with innovative solutions.

Your journal can be a Moleskine, an iPad, a tablet of some sort, an electronic document on your computer, or whatever your heart desires. Small and portable is likely to serve you better. You start each day with a fresh page, symbolizing that each day is a fresh start. You also make room for a capture page to capture items that would otherwise take you off track. After that should come the notes pages for tracking notes from meetings and of your own making. I journal, therefore I am a leader.

Behaviors, Behaviors, Behaviors

Leadership is all wishful thinking unless turned into actual behaviors and then practiced. Get your tools ready and prepare your Immediate Priorities Matrix. Use it to schedule, set expectations, and negotiate. Prepare your End Results Matrix for your leadership goals. Get these on the schedule as well. Start your day and end your day with the journal. Work in bursts. Stop often and get re-energized. Practice the breathing exercise. Practice one behavior at a time. Keep it simple and digestible.

Chapter 3: Leading Strategically—Identifying The Deltas and The Weak Links

Leading strategically in today's information overload

Simple behaviors, big outcomes

I attended an Alexander Techniques workshop recently. The Alexander technique teaches people how to stop using unnecessary levels of muscular and mental tension during their everyday activities. The techniques are very simple and subtle. The impact, though, is quite significant. Just adjusting your head position slightly to release the tension that the neck and back muscles would be otherwise exerting creates a more relaxed feeling. Remembering and practicing these techniques during daily activities multiply the benefits and create a lasting effect.

Many of the behaviors we are practicing here are no different. They are simple and subtle, such as working in focused sessions, working in bursts, using the journal, and taking a few minutes to breathe or stretch. Their impact, however, can be enormous when they are remembered and practiced over time. Our participants report significant outcomes, ranging from feeling less stressed and more fulfilled to achieving breakthrough results.

If you have been reading but are not practicing the behaviors, you're gaining the knowledge but not engaging the emotions. Without the emotions, knowledge remains shallow and temporary. This is like looking at an apple and expecting health benefits. You may be even wondering "What's the big deal?" about these behaviors. The big deal materializes when they are practiced.

Your Leadership Behaviors Mindmap

To facilitate and support these behaviors, several things need to be put in place. This includes insights, such as the impact of interruptions and working in bursts, and skills, such as setting expectations and negotiating, which I will develop further later in the book. This also includes tools, such as the matrices, and techniques, such as use of the journal and the breathing exercise. The diagram below, which I refer to as the Leadership Behaviors Mindmap, shows behaviors in the center and the supporting insights, skills, tools, techniques, and tips:

This is only the beginning. I encourage you to draw your Leadership Behaviors Mindmap and keep adding to it as you learn and practice new ones. Draw the relationships between the behaviors and the supporting insights, skills, tools, techniques, and tips. Expand the Mindmap and personalize it so it reflects your own experiences and discoveries. After all, the relationships in the Mindmap are not one-way relationships. While insights support behaviors, behaviors provide new insights. Along the way, new techniques are discovered. Welcome to the new world of leadership. The possibilities are endless.

The What Worked, What Didn't, and Now What behavior

Leaders don't focus on what didn't work and dwell on it, nor do they focus only on what worked and paint a rosy picture while everyone around them is distressed by the situation, nor do they move quickly to the next thing, ignoring what happened. Instead, they have a balanced view of what worked, what didn't, and what needs to happen next, and they move swiftly to the next action.

Stop often and acknowledge what worked. Even the slightest change or improvement is important. Breakthroughs happen as a result of a series of small improvements. Stop and acknowledge what didn't work. Be curious, factual, and respectful. What didn't work is the hidden gem in which lies real opportunity. This opportunity materializes when you move to the "now what." This means thoughtful action instead of reaction. The "now what" is a remarkable leadership behavior!

"Now what" applies at all levels. Whether it is a project or a task or an issue. Whether it is yours or others'. Whether it is an internal event or an external event over which you had little control. It is also a coaching tool when you work with your team. Depending on the situation, "now what" may result in a tangible action or may end up being an exercise in reflection and learning and then moving on.

The Focusing on Strengths behavior

The philosophy of our leadership program is to focus on strengths—a giant movement in leadership forged by Gallup, Tom Rath, and Barry Conchie, with their StrengthFinder assessment and their *StrengthsFinder 2.0*[4] and *Strengths Based Leadership*[5] books. This may appear to be counterintuitive, because traditionally the focus has been on fixing or eliminating weaknesses. However, when we focus on people's weaknesses, they lose self-confidence, their engagement levels goes down, and they become weaker. This is a guaranteed way to transform a potentially effective team member into a weak and resentful employee.

When we focus on people's strengths, on the other hand, they gain confidence, they get engaged, and they produce great outcomes, and in doing so, they are more likely to overcome their weaknesses.

Recognizing your strengths

An important leadership behavior is recognizing your own strengths, not only so you gain confidence and become more engaged, as we just mentioned, but also because you cannot see other

---

[4] Tom Rath, *StrengthsFinder 2.0* (New York: Gallup Press, 2007)
[5] Tom Rath and Barry Conchie, *Strengths Based Leadership: Great Leaders, Teams, and Why People Follow* (New York: Gallup Press, 2008)

people's strengths unless you are aware of your own. That is exactly why the Strengths Development Plan as an important pillar for our leadership journey.

It may appear to be selfish or even arrogant to be working on acknowledging your own strengths. It is not. It is the best service you can provide to the people around you. We are completely different people and have a completely different presence when we recognize our own strengths.

The sweet spot

If the circle on the left represents the strengths that are necessary to succeed in your current role and the circle on the right represents the strengths that you currently have, then the bigger the intersection, the more likely it is that you will succeed in this role. Additionally, you will be able to perform your responsibilities with ease, therefore feeling less stressed and more accomplished.

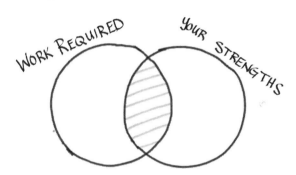

If the third circle below represents the areas that you are passionate about, then the intersection of the three circles is what is referred to as the "sweet spot." Happiness occurs when this sweet spot is large enough to make your work highly fulfilling and fruitful.

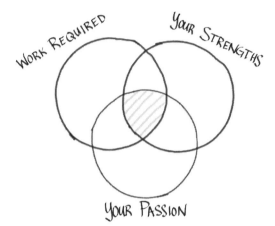

If this intersection between the three circles, however, is non-existent or minimal, this implies that your current role is not a good fit.

Here are some things to reflect on: How do you expand your sweet spot and the sweet spot of your team? What would you do if you or a team member were in a role that is not a good fit? Are you considering the above when hiring, promoting, or assigning roles and responsibilities? Stay tuned for further discussions of these issues.

Deltas and Weak Links: strategic thinking reinvented

You probably have come across the 80/20 rule in some way or another. If you work in sales, for instance, you may have heard or said that 80% of the revenues come from 20% of the customers. If you deal with customer service, you may have heard that 80% of the support issues come from 20% of the users. And there are many more variations. The variation that I am interested in is this: 80% of our results come from 20% of our effort. Yes, 80% of our results come from 20% of our effort.

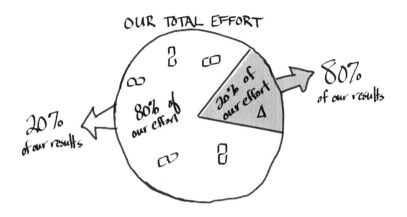

If you are surprised or think this is an exaggeration, do a little experiment. Keep a detailed daily log of every task that you engage in for several days, and then review the log and try to map it to the results that you are trying to accomplish. You are likely to be convinced. The main point is this: Most of what we accomplish comes from certain activities that are closely connected to our desired results. The link between these activities and these results is strong. We refer to these activities as Deltas. And many of the other activities that we perform don't generate much result. The link between these activities and the desired results is weak. We refer to these activities as Weak Links.

The leadership mindset: Is it a Delta or a Weak Link?

Before engaging in any activity, gigantic or miniscule, ask the leadership question: Is this activity a Delta or a Weak Link? This is the leadership mindset. This applies to e-mail, to organizing information, meetings, small projects, big projects—to everything, including interruptions.

If you determine that what you are working on is a Delta, then you are on the right track. Relax. Be happy. This is time well invested. If, however, you determine that this task is a Weak Link, then stop and consider your options. Can you do it faster? Can you reduce its scope? Can you eliminate it altogether?

If you adopt the Delta/Weak Link mindset and apply it often, even if you are moderately successful at it, the outcome is nothing less than phenomenal. If you reduce the time spent on Weak Links by a mere 10%, for instance, and invest this time in Deltas, the increase in results is 40%.

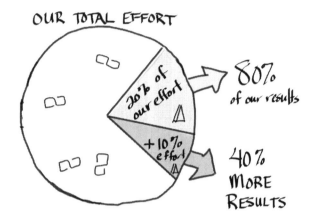

This is a simple mathematical equation: 20% effort produces 80% results; therefore, an increase of 10% effort would produce an extra 40% results. And how much more time did we have to put in to create the 40% increase? None. The total effort, represented by the whole circle, did not change. Getting more accomplished is not about working longer hours; it is about thinking and acting strategically, which translates into reducing the Weak Links and replacing them with Deltas.

How can our results exceed 100%, you might ask? Here is a simple example that shows you how: If you are a salesperson and sell $1M worth of goods this month (100%), it is possible that you will sell $1.2M next month (120%). The 100% (the $1M) represents the current level of results and not the maximum possible results.

Deltas and Weak Links come in different shapes

Weak Links tend to fall into three main categories. First are those activities that we do for historical reasons. It has been done this

37

way for years, so we still do it this way even though the original reason is long gone. Second are those that we do out of avoidance. Instead of directing our effort toward the more challenging Deltas, we keep ourselves busy with the smaller stuff. This helps us feel busy and appear busy. And third are the more legitimate Weak Links, which are supportive activities for our Deltas or others' Deltas.

Deltas also fall into three main categories. First are those that we are doing already and can do more of. Second are those that we are not currently doing, but if we were to do them, we would realize significant gains based on our previous experience or market data. And third are those that we don't know about yet! This last category is an invitation to innovate and discover. This involves research, creativity, market intelligence, questioning, and discovering.

Focus on results—the supreme leadership skill

Make it your mission to identify a specific Weak Link in each of the categories listed and reduce or even eliminate it. Similarly, identify a Delta in each of the described categories, and pursue it relentlessly. Refocus your effort and your team's effort on results. This is leadership at its best. Without focus on results, all effort and skills are diluted and lessened.

What makes this effort challenging is that Deltas and Weak Links aren't as easily distinguishable as one might think. Deltas and Weak Links can be intermixed and intertwined. Therefore, we need to drill down further, dissecting a task into its primary components, examining each component and questioning the value it is contributing to the whole. Once we identify a Weak Link component, we fiercely go after it, ripping it apart and freeing ourselves and our team from its burden.

True leaders are conscious of not delegating Weak Links. If it is a Weak Link, it should be eliminated instead of delegated and turned into someone else's burden. Furthermore, leaders need to coach their teams on adopting the Delta/Weak Link mindset and give them the freedom to act. Two important questions need to be posed to identify whether a task or a component is a Delta or a Weak Link. First, which result is it contributing to? Having identified the desired results is therefore a prerequisite for strategic thinking. If you identify the result to which your task is contributing, then you should ask some other questions: Is your task contributing significantly to this result? Or is there a better way to get to this result?

Time Management reinvented for leaders

Identify the Deltas. Focus on the Deltas. Set expectations for Weak Links that don't get done. In today's overload, it is likely that you have too much to do and too little time to do it. If your goal is to get things done, you are likely to be frustrated, overwhelmed, and unsuccessful. Or if you are successful, it's at the expense of your well-being.

If you're not going to do everything there is to do, it would be better to do the Deltas and let some Weak Links remain undone, as opposed to the other way around! The paradox is that when you get Deltas done, you feel energized and accomplished and able to bulldoze your way through Weak Links like never before. Take this approach a step further. Create a not-to-do list. Include Weak Links that you consciously decide to not do. Be bold! Be a leader.

Focus reinvented for leaders

Focus is highly desired by many. However, it remains elusive for most. It is time to demystify it and translate it into practical behaviors that you can practice. Focus needs to be practiced at three levels: micro focus, macro focus, and process focus. Let us embark on this journey, which has the potential to transform your life, when practiced consistently.

Micro Focus

Micro focus has to do with our thought processes and the ability to stay focused on one train of thought in order to accomplish a meaningful outcome. Our minds, however, tend to be scattered and tend to wander. Our own wandering thoughts are by far the primary cause for interruptions in our tasks, derailing us into new and often unrelated territories.

Imagine me working on budget projections for the quarter. As I try to think about how much I should allow for online advertisement, my gaze drifts up while I contemplate what the right number might be. My gaze settles on the photo on my desk: me in Paris. What a lovely trip that was last year. Except for the price of gas. I can remember that gas station where I stopped to fill up. I can see the numbers flashing past ninety euros. No question Hertz should be renting hybrids or electrics. I then start browsing the Internet for the next ten to twenty minutes to see if anyone is renting hybrids in Europe. Suddenly, I realize that I am way off track and ask myself the question, "What the heck was I working on?"

Focusing on Task A

I call any work we are trying to accomplish Task A. Task A represents the work that is our most important work. It's what we want to do. It's what our team wants us to do, too. If we do all our Task A's, we accomplish all of our life's desires. Accomplishment lies in racking up those Task A's. Ideally, in the Accomplishment Zone™, we would focus on Task A and perform activities related to it until Task A is finished or until we've at least made significant progress on it.

In essence, our well-behaved mind would only have thoughts related to Task A, which are shown in the diagram below as Thoughts A1, A2, and A3.

Promoting Killer B

Unfortunately, reality tends to be a little different from this ideal. Typically, soon after we start working on Task A, Thought B comes along. What in the world is Thought B doing here? Who knows, but it's here. What do we do when thought B comes along?

As shown below, more often than not, when Thought B comes along, we are likely to get kidnapped by it. We shift our line of thinking to Thought B while abandoning Task A. Thought B is a threat to continuing to work on our goal, which is Task A. Thought B is dangerous. Thought B is, in fact, a Killer B. Seriously? A kind of thought so bad, I call it a "killer"? Yes. It's that bad.

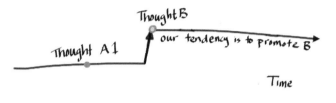

When we give our attention to Thought B and begin to think about what it means, begin to make associations for it, and begin to play with it, we let Thought B take over our consciousness. Until we can regain control of our senses, we have abandoned work on Thought A and Task A.

Capturing Killer B

What options do we have other than promoting Killer B? What would be a more constructive option? We could "capture" Killer B, so we can free our mind from it and return to it later if necessary.

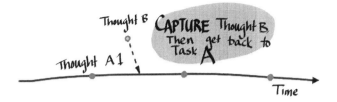

Where do we capture Killer B's? This calls for a new page in the leader's journal: the Capture page. This means that in addition to the Today page in the journal, where we jot down what we intended to accomplish today, we need another page for capturing Killer B's and other interruptions that come along.

Ignoring Killer B

Are all thoughts worth capturing? Thankfully, not. Otherwise, some of us would spend most of our time capturing the multitude of thoughts that keep popping up in our busy and creative minds. If we determine that Killer B is just a random thought and is not worth capturing because its future value is insignificant, it makes more sense to ignore it and get back to Task A as soon as possible, as illustrated below:

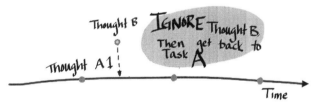

Turning Killer B into Useful B

It is possible that Killer B proves not to be a "killer" after all. It may be that Killer B has some value to add to Task A. This is actually the way the mind works sometimes. It unexpectedly produces an interesting thought that may not be directly related to Task A but has some correlation to it and some applicable insights. In this case, it is best to integrate the useful aspects of Killer B into Task A and therefore turn Killer B into Useful B, as illustrated below:

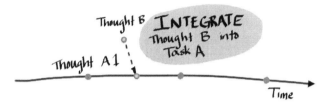

How Do We Stay Focused?

First Technique: Using a timer

Not any timer—a countdown timer. Setting the countdown timer for forty minutes (or whatever time period we choose) and then pushing the Start button has significant implications.

Just the fact that the timer is running seems to drastically heighten our awareness of time and allow us to quickly notice when we deviate from our task. It's as simple as that.

The Timer Creates Purpose

The timer helps us put a stake in the ground and declare that we have officially started the task at hand. Without such a clear signal, it is easy to stay noncommittal, starting one task but then casually withdrawing from it to start another one. It is possible to keep testing task after task, escaping from the ones that are more difficult or less desirable and sneaking into tasks that are easier (and, just as likely, less crucial). I call this "task hopping"!

The Timer Creates Accountability

In addition to creating purpose, the timer also creates accountability. Now that the timer has started, in forty minutes we are going to know clearly if we accomplished what we intended. The timer also helps us estimate time better in the future. Knowing how long it takes to accomplish any given project in such a time-crunched era is a rare and highly desirable skill.

The timer prompts us to move things forward

During the focused session, the timer improves the quality and efficiency of our work. It prompts us to face the issues, make decisions, and move things along as opposed to dwelling on issues and staying indefinitely in analysis/paralysis mode. In other words, the timer accelerates our pace.

The timer as a stress relief mechanism

The timer signifies that we have given ourselves permission to be where we are for the time period we have chosen. Now we can more easily give up the guilt or anxiety that we would otherwise experience for not being somewhere else and not handling all the other things that need to be handled.

The happy sound of accomplishment

The happy sound of accomplishment is only minutes away, and when it is heard or seen (when the timer goes off), we are likely to experience a range of thoughts and feelings, the most prevalent of which is likely to be satisfaction. Stopping is critical at this juncture. Even a brief moment of acknowledgement—celebrating that something has been accomplished—goes a long way.

Second Technique: Micro-Planning™

Micro-Planning™ consists of creating a brief outline at the beginning of your focused session, listing key steps that need to get done in order to complete the selected task, such as:

Task	Update projections
Micro-Plan™	Download the latest spreadsheet
	Review the most recent guidelines
	Update the formulas accordingly
	Regenerate PivotTables and graphs
	Upload updated version
	Schedule meeting to review with team

The Micro-Plan™ calls for a new set of pages in the journal; I refer to these pages as the Notes pages. These pages are also useful for regular note-taking, strategizing, and visual thinking. Your leader's journal is evolving. It now includes the Today page, the Capture page, and one or more Notes pages. Every day is a fresh start. You flip to a new page and jot down the date and what you intend to accomplish on this day (the Today page). Next, you assign the following page for capturing interruptions (the Capture page). Finally, you assign the first Notes page and continue to add Notes pages as needed.

Just like the timer, which appears to be a simple and perhaps expendable tool on the surface, Micro-Planning™ is a powerful technique that can help us stay focused. And if and when we have to deviate to take care of urgent issues, the Micro-Plan™ helps us restart our task with the minimum amount of effort and the fastest recovery time.

As we get deeper into our task, the Micro-Plan™ can continue to evolve and serve as the short-term parking lot for new potential steps or related ideas that would otherwise derail us from the current steps. Our mind stays fully available for the core issues we are processing now. The Micro-Plan™ and the journal become our thinking pad, as well as the extension of and support system for our short-term memory, which is challenged by information continually and relentlessly invading our mind space. Micro-Planning™ and the timer work together to help achieve focus, purpose, and results that will add up to meaningful accomplishments.

Third Technique: Turning Off External Interruptions

It sounds simple, and it would be, if all external interruptions were within our control. Wishful thinking! Indeed, we can turn off the e-mail beep, forward the phone to voicemail, and indicate that we are busy or "away" in our Instant Messaging status (which we should do during our focus sessions). But it is much more difficult to switch off the people who stop by, the noise or conversations around our work area, and, most importantly, the urgent and critical requests that come from bosses, colleagues, customers, family and friends. In addition, we become mentally distracted by the blame and guilt that come from not being available to handle all of the above promptly.

The answer to these external challenges is certainly not simple, but it is an area where we have more influence than we tend to believe. To better manage these group-inflicted interruptions, it is imperative to (a) find an agreed-upon way to communicate to our team that we are focused (whether it is putting up a sign in our work area or setting our IM status appropriately) and (b) find an agreed-upon way for our team to escalate critical issues to us when such issues come up (whether it is cell phone, pager, or a special keyword in IM).

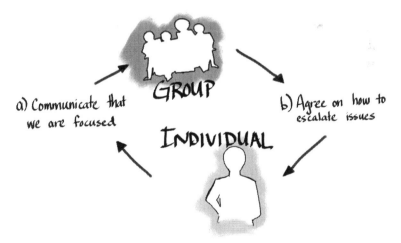

The answer also lies in negotiating effectively with the world to help align goals and priorities and to optimize how responsibilities and tasks are divided and distributed. Using collaboration technologies is essential in this effort, as is developing best practices around these technologies so they support us instead of hindering us.

Macro Focus

Macro focus refers to focusing on the Deltas. While micro focus is highly desirable—without it our effort is diluted and not likely to add up to significant results—it is only by combining micro focus with macro focus and carefully choosing precisely *what* to focus on that we achieve successful outcomes. Leaders grasp that macro focus and micro focus work hand in hand and that one without the other is fruitless.

Process Focus

Process focus refers to the Results Curve and to working in bursts. While micro focus and macro focus are essential, without alternating between focus, collaboration, and playtime, we can become isolated, uncooperative, and experience burnout. Focus becomes worthwhile when we skillfully combine the three levels of focus, from micro to macro to process.

Focus and leadership

Give your team the time to focus and therefore create results! Nothing is more motivating and confidence building than achieving meaningful results. Enable your team to work in bursts and coach them to work on the Deltas. Educate them about micro focus. After all, one of the primary purposes of leading is creating results through people, while helping them develop and feel fulfilled. With the three levels of focus, results can be created and people feel successful and fulfilled. Otherwise, everyone is spinning their wheels mostly in place and without impact. Focus and leadership go hand in hand in today's workplace.

The leader's day, augmented

We established earlier that a leader's day starts with a moment of reflection, identifying what the leader intends to accomplish that day, and that the leader's day ends with a moment of reflection on what was accomplished, what lessons were learned, and what still needs to be accounted for and reconciled. We also established that the journal, paper or electronic, is the leader's companion throughout the day.

Augment your use of the journal. When you experience an aha moment as a result of trying a new leadership behavior, make a note of it in your journal. Create a leadership sidebar to track these moments and thus strengthen and cement the underlying thoughts and feelings. These small moments add up and result in quantum leaps. New branches between the neurons in your brain continue to form and get reinforced. You are basically building a leadership brain with no surgery and no drugs needed. It is all through your natural ability to choose and behave differently. You are also accumulating leadership "capital" that you can leverage in crucial moments.

Keep augmenting your use of the journal. Create another sidebar to track your wellness-related behaviors. This can be your physical exercise, nutrition related information, breathing, meditating, and breaks. Dare to evolve the use of the journal and take it to new levels. This is your leadership journal.

The leader's calendar

An equally important tool for leading effectively is the calendar. A typical calendar shows back-to-back meetings. This doesn't leave time for leading and certainly not strategic thinking, strategic action, or coaching, among other leadership behaviors. One behavior that can help undo this unfortunate workplace phenomenon is blocking time on the calendar for important tasks, projects, and initiatives, including thinking, coaching, and rejuvenating. The calendar is the only visual representation of time. If something is not on the calendar, it is not visible and not in the forefront. The calendar is also a shared resource, and it communicates how committed our time is. Let your Immediate Priorities Matrix and your End Results Matrix help you bring what is important to the forefront and help you communicate through your calendar.

The leader's e-mail

If you are still in e-mail jail, it is time you free yourself! You have the key, in the form of a few simple behaviors. A leader's day can't possibly be driven and controlled by e-mail, because a leader works in bursts. In the focused burst, the leader is concentrating on Delta effort and therefore e-mail takes a back seat or is thrown out of the window. Following the focused burst comes the collaboration burst, which starts with an e-mail burst.

An e-mail burst is intensely focused on e-mail, mostly on Delta e-mails, while swiftly sweeping through other e-mails. The leader's e-mail inbox also looks different. E-mails don't just sit around and claim residency. Once an e-mail is read, it is either handled and moved away, or if it can't be handled, it is immediately assigned a timeframe in which it needs to be handled, with specially designated categories, tags, or labels. This timeframe can be today, tomorrow, or a specific timeframe with a reminder. Delegated messages are tracked with their own category so they are easily findable. Leaders know at all times what e-mails they need to handle today and what e-mails are waiting for others to answer.

Behaviors, Behaviors, Behaviors

You realize by now that leadership is all wishful thinking unless turned into actual behaviors and then practiced. Practice appreciating and acknowledging people's strengths. When you do so, keep it simple and authentic. Pay attention to what others are doing well, and give them recognition for it. Don't limit yourself. In addition to practicing this with your colleagues and direct reports, practice it also with your manager and others in your organization. Take it home and practice it with your family and friends. How about with service clerks or waitstaff at restaurants and cafes? If you already give praise to people often, try to do it differently! Make it more specific. Give it only when it is truly deserved.

Review your Immediate Priorities Matrix from earlier with the Deltas and Weak Links in mind. Find ways to reduce the time spent on Weak Links or even eliminate some. Review your End Results Matrix and determine if the projects, initiatives, and activities that you put down are the most effective ways to get to the desired goals. See if you can come up with more effective ways to reach these goals.

Stop several times a day to do the Delta/Weak Link check. If you find that you happen to be engaged in a Weak Link, limit the scope of this task or eliminate it altogether. You can choose to delegate the task, but only if you can find someone who can do it more efficiently than you can or whose role and strengths are better suited to this task. Leaders don't just randomly delegate Weak Links, which simply creates inefficiencies and waste.

When you get interrupted, and before you take that interruption, put it through the Delta/Weak Link test. Remember that you can diplomatically say no to the interruption or postpone it by jotting it down on your Capture page.

Chapter 4: Leading In Today's Social World

Fatal Flaw

Before we dive into the social world, let us consider one important aspect to the strengths concept. I have been talking about strengths and, so far, have ignored weaknesses. It is time to talk about a specific type of weakness that John Zenger refers to as the "fatal flaw"!

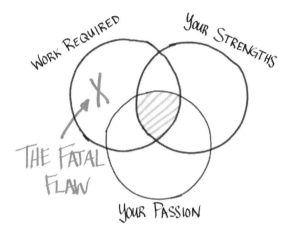

As shown above, a fatal flaw is a strength that your work requires but that you don't currently have. It is not just that you don't have this strength, but it happens to be critical for being successful in your current role. This may be because of the nature of your work or because of the work environment and culture.

If you are not aware of a fatal flaw and therefore never do anything about it, it is likely that it will limit your success and make your work overly difficult and unfulfilling. For instance, you may find yourself in an entrepreneurial environment where flexibility and adaptability to constantly changing priorities are highly valued keys to success. However, you may have been brought on board because of your subject matter expertise, and you happen to value relationship building and structure and are not comfortable with unexpected changes. Your inability to be flexible and to adapt to constant change is a fatal flaw in this role.

A few questions that can help you discern whether you have a fatal flaw: Are you finding work really difficult? Do other people

53

in a similar position find things much easier than you do? Are you getting feedback that might be pointing to a fatal flaw but that you are ignoring or dismissing?

If you identify a fatal flaw situation, then comes the "now what" question, which is one of the leadership behaviors we discussed previously. While this situation may be upsetting and discouraging at first, it can potentially be turned into an opportunity. You might address this flaw through informal and formal learning so you acquire the skills needed in this area. This can turn into an exciting and rewarding endeavor, in which you explore classes, events, and associations and possibly find a mentor or a coach. Remember that our brain is not fixed; it can be rewired.

Alternatively, you might find someone to complement you and fill in the gap. If you are in a leadership position, identify someone on your team who has that strength. If no one does, make this your next goal when you recruit people.

Ultimately if this is an area where learning or partnering with someone is not possible or desirable, then it is time for change. This doesn't necessarily mean leaving your current job or organization. It may constitute negotiating and redefining your role.

If you identify a fatal flaw, go through the "now what" analysis and identify your strategy. This discussion of fatal flaws also applies to your staff. When you realize that someone on your team is in this situation, it is time you approach the situation head on with the "now what" analysis. Identifying a strategy and supporting this person in overcoming such a difficult situation is a sign of leadership.

Social Media Survey Results

Before I discuss social media and its implication on business and leadership, I would like to share with you the results of a survey that my team and I did about how business professionals use social media, in which 1000 people participated. Here are the survey questions and results.

1. Which of the following "inboxes" do you check regularly?

About the question: This question is intended to see how many of these platforms have become part of the daily life of the participants. This was made a multiple-choice question to allow the participants to select multiple platforms. A result such as 92.1% (see "Personal e-mail" in the graph below) indicates that 92.1% of the participants checked their personal e-mail regularly.

The survey results:

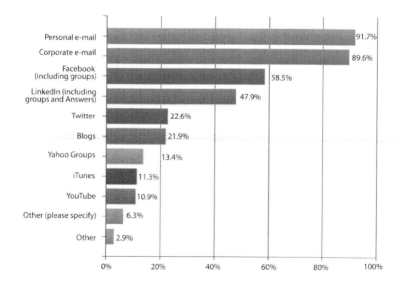

2. Which best describes how you handle these "inboxes" (those defined above)?

About the question: This question is intended to highlight two aspects. First, how many of our participants are still mostly pre-occupied with e-mail (the more traditional inbox, as we know it) and not yet monitoring social media much? Second, for those who are monitoring e-mail and social media (what I call the New Inbox), how frequently did they monitor them (most of the time, or only some of the time)? Overall this question is intended to show how entrenched social media has become in our lives (in this case mostly work life, but also an indication of how entrenched it is now in our personal life).

The survey results:

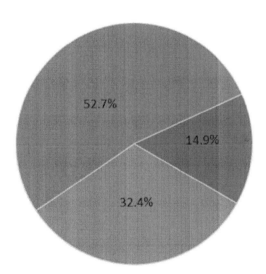

▬ Monitor only e-mail
▬ Monitor multiple "inboxes" most of the time
▬ Monitor multiple "inboxes" from time to time

3. How well do you think you are managing and leveraging your "inboxes"?

About the question: This is a self-assessment of how the participants believe they manage and leverage their e-mail and social media activities (the New Inbox). This question relates to two correlated but distinct aspects: *managing* and *leveraging*. It is partly a question of how satisfied they are with the way they are working with e-mail and social media (the managing part), and it is partly a question of whether they are getting the most out of it and seeing some results (the leveraging part).

The survey results:

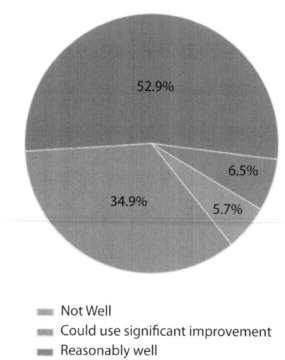

- ▬ Not Well
- ▬ Could use significant improvement
- ▬ Reasonably well
- ▬ Extremely well

4. Do you have a strategy behind how you manage your "inboxes" or do you do it in an ad-hoc fashion?

About the question: This question goes beyond the self-assessment question above, exploring the degree to which the participants are "strategic" in using e-mail and social media. This reflects how well they have thought through their use of e-mail and social media. The more they've thought it through (i.e., those who have a defined strategy), the more likely their activities are leading to more measurable business results. The more ad-hoc they are in their usage, the less likely they will get such results.

The survey results:

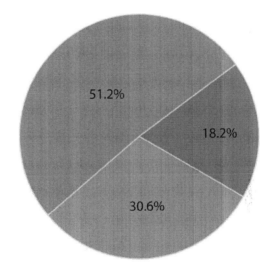

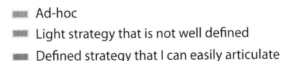

▬ Ad-hoc
▬ Light strategy that is not well defined
▬ Defined strategy that I can easily articulate

5. What tools (software tools, add-on applications, mobile devices) are you using to help you manage these "inboxes"?

About the question: This question intends to identify the key tools that participants are using in managing e-mail and social media. This question was asked as a free-form question to allow participants to indicate a broad range of tools and not limit or direct their choices. The graph below indicates the most common tools that the participants mentioned in their answers.

The survey results:

6. How often do you interrupt your work to check your "inboxes"?

About the question: While question 2 above identifies how entrenched e-mail and social media are in our daily work life, and question 3 identifies how satisfied we are with managing and leveraging these platforms, and question 4 explores how strategic we are in using them and therefore how likely it is that our usage is aligned with our business results, question 6 focuses on the core issue of interruptions and therefore productivity. This question is intended to explore how serious this problem is and how the New Inbox is contributing to it.

The survey results:

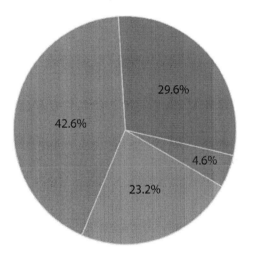

- Constantly as soon as new information shows up
- More often than I would like to
- From time to time but not excessively
- Rarely

7. Your function?

About the question: This question is intended to identify the roles that our participants play at their organizations, therefore allowing us to report on how the trends vary by function and examine if there are noticeable differences. The actual results by function are included in a later chapter in this book.

The survey results:

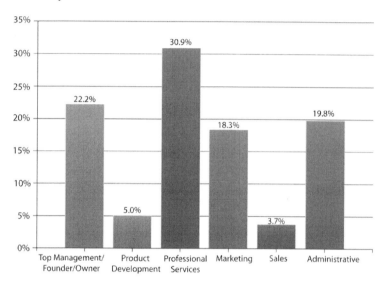

8. Your status?

About the question: This question is intended to identify the size of the companies at which our participants work, therefore allowing us to report on how the trends vary by company size and examine if there are noticeable differences. The actual results by function are included in a later chapter in the book.

The survey results:

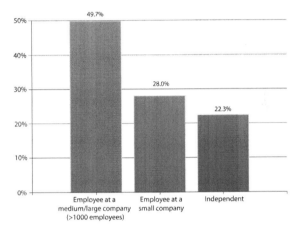

9. How much time do you spend on your "inboxes" per day?

About the question: This question is intended to measure the amount of time spent on e-mail and social media and therefore quantify how entrenched these platforms have become in our work life. This question also compares e-mail to the social media platforms.

The survey results:

	Less than 30 minutes	Up to 1 hour	Up to 2 hours	Up to 4 hours	Most of the day
E-mail	5.1%	20.6%	33.6%	21.9%	18.8%
Social Media	53.2%	27.4%	12.4%	4.1%	2.9%

10. How much of your social media is for work versus personal reasons?

About the question: This question is intended to identify how much of the social media effort is for business versus personal reasons. It is exploring how many of our participants think of these platforms as business tools versus tools for personal socializing and leisure.

The survey results:

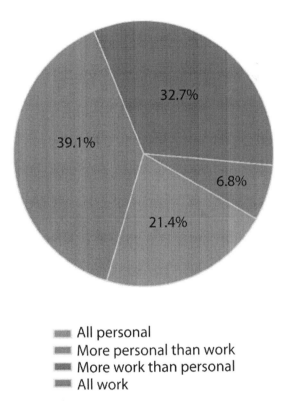

- ▬ All personal
- ▬ More personal than work
- ▬ More work than personal
- ▬ All work

11. Your generation?

About the question: This question is intended to identify generations that our participants belong to, therefore allowing us to report on how the trends vary by generation and examine if there are noticeable differences. The actual results by generation are included in a later chapter in this book.

The survey results:

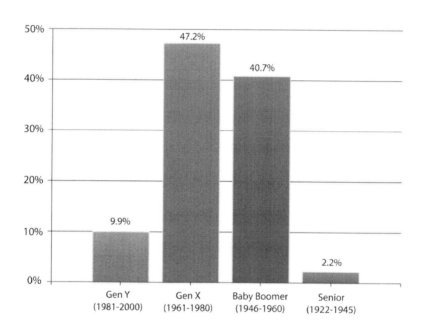

12 to 15. Myers-Briggs Type Indicator if you happen to know it?

About the question: This question intends to identify the Myers-Briggs Type Indicator[6] of the participants. The graphs below display the results in each of the four main areas of the Myers-Briggs Type Indicator.

The survey results:

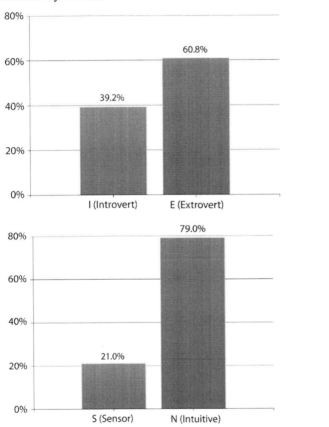

---

[6] Refer to http://www.myersbriggs.org/ for more information about the Myers-Briggs Type Indicator®

Myers-Briggs Type Indicator (continued)

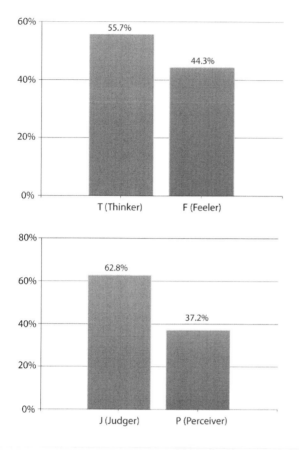

Key Findings and Conclusions

Here are the nine key findings and conclusions from the survey results:

E-mail is still king and its usage still outweighs social media by three to one; we are caught in an e-mail vortex, a death-trap, and no one knows how to escape

Business professionals spend an average of 3.27 hours per day on e-mail and 1.18 hours on social media. While social media has become an integral part of our daily work life and has gained significant adoption, e-mail is still by far the number one inbox that business professionals go to. Facebook comes next, and then LinkedIn. Twitter has not gained as much traction among our participants, except for Gen Y users who seem to use Twitter more so than other generations and more so than LinkedIn.

This shows that we continue to be the creators and victims of the e-mail overload. While the younger generations are less attached to e-mail, the multi-generational workplace is still dependent on it. This pervasive reliance on e-mail is an indication that productivity suffers and knowledge within the organization is neither shared nor leveraged properly, thus continuing to be fragmented and unharnessed. In addition to this are the resulting challenges that IT, HR, and Operations have to deal with, ranging from security, spam, storage, archiving, and network performance to confidentiality, privacy, copyright and trademark infringement, plus potential claims of discrimination and abuse.

Social media is on the rise and future generations will redefine its use in the workplace; however, today social media is misused and contributing little to productivity and business results

The use of social media in the workplace is developing rapidly with 58.5% of the survey participants checking Facebook regularly, 47.9% checking LinkedIn regularly, 22.6% checking Twitter, and 21.9% reading blogs. Younger generations lead the pack in their use of Social Media with Gen Y spending an average of 1.8 hours per day on it, compared to 1.21 hours for Gen X, 1 hour for Baby Boomers, and 0.59 hour for Seniors. The time spent on social media, however, is more for personal reasons than work reasons, with only 6.8% of the participants indicating that they use social media solely for work purposes. In addition, only 18.2% of the participants indicate that they have a defined strategy, and only 5.7% believe that they are managing and leveraging their effort very well.

Therefore the outlook of social media at work is currently grim. While we have adopted social media and use it regularly, we are still at the very early stages of learning its applications at work and starting to transfer our learning from the social to business context. The younger generations are more likely to be the ones who speed up this transfer and redefine the use of these platforms in the workplace. Until that happens, social media remains a costly distraction and adds significantly to the risks and costs that IT, HR, and Operations have to address.

Workplace interruptions pose a real threat to productivity and are far more significant than expected; the New Inbox threatens to shrink the bottom line

Most participants check these inboxes too often and are constantly interrupting their work to do so. About one-quarter of the survey participants (23.2%) indicated that they check their inboxes as soon as new information shows up, and more than one-third of the participants (another 42.6%) admitted that they interrupt their work more often than they would like.

This indicates enormous losses in productivity for companies. Not only do those interruptions take time, but the recovery time that it takes to get back on track is even more significant. Considering the 4.45 hours per day that two-thirds of the workforce is spending inefficiently, from one interruption to the next, the direct cost is of the magnitude of one-third of the total payroll for a company. The resulting opportunity cost is incalculable.

Tremendous opportunities exist for tools that can help streamline and "socialize" e-mail, manage interruptions, and take information off of e-mail to more appropriate information sharing technologies

With an average of 3.27 hours per day spent on e-mail and most users habitually interrupting their work to check e-mail, it is evident that current e-mail technologies do not adequately enable or facilitate efficient user practices. Furthermore, current information sharing technologies don't integrate well with e-mail and have not achieved significant adoption.

Tremendous opportunities exist for e-mail technologies that can help users track the time spent on e-mail, provide metrics on usage, shield users from e-mail interruptions, manage presence, and provide elaborate rules and notification capabilities. Opportunities also exist for "socializing" e-mail by (a) allowing e-mail recipients to rank and comment on the content and relevance of e-mail messages and (b) providing better integration of e-mail with internal and external social media platforms. In addition, opportunities exist for e-mail technologies and information sharing technologies to have seamless integration points to enable users to easily tag and publish information from e-mail to more persistent and widely shared documents, wikis, blogs, and similar repositories.

Social media has shattered the divide between business and personal use while creating further divides between generations in the workplace, between functional areas, and between companies of various sizes

The vast majority of the survey participants (71.8%) use social media for both work and personal reasons. Social media seems to have significantly reduced the divide between what is work and what is personal, and enabled, or even encouraged, personal and business networks to merge during and after work hours. However, when we look at how different generations use social media (platforms, tools, time spent, how strategically, etc.), it seems that social media amplifies the generational differences, especially between Gen Y and Baby Boomers. In addition, sales and marketing professionals seem to have adopted social media significantly more than top management or administrative professionals. When it comes to company size, employees of smaller companies (less than 1000 employees) seem to have adopted social media more than employees of larger companies (more than 1000 employees). All in all, it seems that a social media divide has developed, resulting in two segments: one consisting of the social media savvy and engaged professionals and the other of the social media ambivalent or even avoidant.

Tremendous opportunities also exist for tools that can help the enterprise better manage the use of social media, both internally and externally, and link social media efforts to business goals

The use of social media tools is largely fragmented. Most participants use a broad range of social media tools that are not enterprise enabled. Tremendous opportunities exist for enterprise tools that can help (a) bring the social media-like features to the workplace, allowing business professionals to connect, share information, collaborate and co-create with their team members, as well as with distributed groups across the organization and (b) allow business professionals to leverage the external social media platforms in their current projects by tapping into broader networks for market research, marketing, customer service, and more.

Vendors are starting to offer these tools (Jive Software, Telligent Systems Community Server, Cisco Quad, Salesforce.com Chatter, IBM Lotus Connections, Microsoft SharePoint Social Sites by NewsGator, Mzinga Social Media Suite, and many others) but these tools are in their early stages and the adoption is still minimal, as shown in the survey results. These tools will help direct the use of social media toward work-related purposes and also reduce the divide between generations and functions.

There is a dire need for education and awareness programs relating to the use of e-mail and social media in the workplace, as well as for mentoring and reverse mentoring between generations

With employees spending 4.45 hours per day on e-mail and social media, and knowing the risks and costs associated with the use of e-mail and social media in the workplace—as well as the untapped potential of these platforms (in market research, customer service, sales and marketing, recruiting, and more)—the need for education and awareness programs is evident.

While these costs and risks are not new, nor is the need for education and awareness, they all have been considerably augmented by social media and the fact that it shattered the divide between business and personal use, increasing work interruptions and unproductive time. As a prerequisite to these educational and awareness programs, there needs to be a clear and up-to-date e-

71

policy put in place. Leveraging the social media savvy employees (such as Gen Y and those in Marketing) during this effort and allowing them to mentor others can help bridge the divide, resulting in increased collaboration and reducing the cost of these programs.

E-mail marketing is still the primary online marketing vehicle, and e-mail marketing programs and tools that integrate social media marketing are likely to be the winners

With e-mail still king and business users still on e-mail more than any other social media platform, e-mail is still the most effective way to reach those users. However, considering that e-mail has been excessively used by marketers and e-mail users are fatigued from marketing messages, in addition to the fact that the use of social media is on the rise, there is an opportunity for e-mail programs and marketing tools to more fully integrate social media capabilities. These platforms can thus be leveraged to get through to their target audiences and create lasting relationships with them in the social media platforms. The same applies to sales programs and tools and the opportunity to integrate them with the social media platforms. Considering that social media use is about one-third of e-mail usage already—and this trend is likely to continue—the investment in social media as compared to e-mail needs to match that.

A major technological revolution is on its way; it is the creation of a wholly integrated *New* New Inbox platform, which will reshape workplace communication and information sharing

Looking at the serious challenges that are emphasized by the survey results, the costs and risks associated with these challenges, and the tremendous opportunities that exist for e-mail and social media in the workplace, I predict that the future will bring a new kind of platform—the integrated *New* New Inbox platform—that will (a) integrate e-mail and social media, (b) provide both internal social media capabilities within the enterprise and access to external social media platforms, (c) socialize e-mail with tagging, ranking, and seamless linking to social media feeds and information sharing repositories, (d) integrate "search" and include both external and internal results, (e) provide metrics and feedback on individual and group usage to measure effort and assess relevance to business results, (f) integrate both personal and work effort, (g) be simple, intuitive, and elegant, and (h) be secure and cloud-based, to function from anywhere and on any device and any OS platform.

This revolution has already started and is likely to be fulfilled by Gen Y and future generations, who have migrated away from e-mail and think differently about communication and information sharing. This revolution is likely to be managed and guided by members of Gen X, who have adopted the new paradigm of social media more fully than Baby Boomers. This New New Inbox will capture the eyes of the future and will exceed Google and Facebook, which will play a part but not necessarily dominate.

Opportunities, Challenges, and Recommendations

What does it all mean for business and leadership? The 3x3 COS Formula below offers the related insights and actions that business leaders need to be aware of and consider.

The 3x3 COS Formula

This formula is my simplified version of the SWOT analysis, the strategic planning method used to evaluate the Strengths, Weaknesses, Opportunities, and Threats involved in a project or in a business. However the 3x3 COS formula, unlike SWOT, adds an additional component, which are the steps that need to be taken as a result of the analysis.

The 3x3 COS formula consists of analyzing and identifying the (a) Challenges, (b) Opportunities, and (c) Steps that need to be taken, relating to a new trend or change in the overall market conditions, specific technology, social behavior, or whatever the issue at hand is. It is intended to identify up to three items only in each of these areas and therefore stay focused on the critical elements that are most likely to generate the highest returns.

The 3x3 COS formula answers the important "now what" question that sometimes research leaves unanswered. For instance, in this survey report, we learned a great deal about the current state and potential trends relating to the use of e-mail and social media in the workplace, but if we don't translate these to specific steps that we can take, it is not likely that we will benefit as much from this knowledge. The 3x3 COS formula is designed to prompt us to think through our findings, come up with practical applications for them, and motivate us to take the necessary next steps. It is the cure for research addiction and the analysis/paralysis syndrome.

The 3x3 COS Formula Applied to the Use of E-mail and Social Media in the Workplace

Knowing that my focus is on productivity in the workplace and helping companies and their employees get more accomplished in today's information overload, my analysis is centered on productivity and collaboration. However, you can find analysis from other angles by industry and business leaders, who will be contributing their 3x3 COS Formula analyses about the use of e-mail and social media in the workplace, at the Less-Is-More blog (http://www.people-onthego.com/blog).

The Top Three Challenges

Time

The time spent on e-mail and social media is phenomenal. Time translates into direct cost and to opportunity cost. This challenge is difficult to tackle. It is difficult because this time is spent in very small increments and goes unnoticed. If people were to go away for two weeks at a time every month to work on e-mail and social media (which is the equivalent of the actual time spent on these platforms, according to the survey results), this would be perceived as catastrophic and companies would put a ban on e-mail and social media. But knowing that this time is spent in increments of minutes here and there, it is easily dismissed, difficult to measure, and difficult to act upon.

Another difficulty is that everyone, from top management to each individual contributor, is guilty of spending this time. Furthermore, it is nobody's responsibility to monitor this time. All things considered, no one will blow the whistle. Finally, what makes this issue difficult to tackle is that there is no simple solution. So what is the point of blowing the whistle? It is a multi-faceted problem that requires intervention at all levels. It is a huge problem that gradually and quietly grew. (This is known as the boiled frog phenomenon.)

Interruptions

It is not just the time but how this time is spent. Interruptions are the 800-pound gorilla in the room. They are just as difficult to tackle as the time challenge and for the same reasons stated above. The Results Curve™ estimates that interruptions can actually diminish our results to a small fraction of the potential results that we would get if we were to eliminate those interruptions (a shocking 10 to 20 percent of the potential results).

It is not just the interruption itself but also the recovery time needed after an interruption. When we resume our work after an interruption, our mind needs to re-retrieve the relevant pieces of information that were let go during the interruption and reconstruct the logic and relationships that were previously established. This means that we suffer a serious setback and need a considerable amount of recovery time. With the majority of the workforce constantly or often interrupting their own work, as shown in the survey results, to check e-mail and social media, as well as interrupting others by sending unnecessary or poorly written e-mails and social media posts, this is like an avalanche that is wiping out a significant chunk of corporate productivity.

Inappropriate use

Inappropriate use ranges from non-strategic use on one end to inappropriate content and security breaches that can cause significant legal and IT risks on the other. Non-strategic use is the use of e-mail and social media in ways that aren't aligned with business goals and therefore causing this effort to contribute minimal returns. With only 18.2 percent of the participants having a clearly defined strategy behind their use of e-mail and social media, it is clear that this challenge is substantial. In addition, with more time spent on social media and more of it on personal use than business use, the legal and IT risks are more significant than ever before.

Content posted casually on social media platforms that mentions work colleagues or work-related issues may end up leading to discrimination claims, exposing confidential information, and being a misuse of copyrighted material. Inappropriate use can also cause degradation in network performance issues and increased risks of network viruses and related problems.

I wonder if the most significant inappropriate use is using the incorrect medium for the given task; for example, sending e-mail when a phone call would be infinitely more effective, or tweeting when LinkedIn or Facebook might serve better.

We've all watched people spend hours writing e-mail messages, when simple phone calls would be more efficient and less prone to misunderstanding. Or, if proximity permits, you can't beat a face-to-face conversation.

The Top Three Opportunities

Companies to embrace social media to increase collaboration and extend their reach

The same way social media revolutionized communication and networking in public platforms, it can do the same within the enterprise and transform how business professionals build relationships, share information, innovate, and execute on strategic projects, initiatives, and business ventures internally. Externally, there are some unique opportunities for companies to enhance and extend their marketing, sales, and customer service effort, using social media. There is also the opportunity to leverage the employees' social networks, which would help extend the company's reach in the public social media platforms.

Employees to become more social media savvy and more strategic in their use of e-mail and social media

Employees have tremendous opportunities to help their companies and their careers by enhancing their social media skills and developing effective strategies for their e-mail and social media effort. Being social media savvy is a skill that will enhance performance in virtually any job responsibility and is likely to create unique career opportunities in the future. And with e-mail continuing to be the leading communication vehicle at work, using it strategically is not only a necessity to help manage the overload, but an ability that will emerge as a leadership skill that is required and expected of tomorrow's leaders, managers, and supervisors.

Vendors to bring some innovative e-mail and social media tools

As suggested in the Key Findings in chapter 3, tremendous opportunities exist for e-mail technologies that can help users track the time spent on e-mail, provide metrics on usage, shield users from e-mail interruptions, manage presence, and provide elaborate rules and notifications capabilities. Opportunities also exist for "socializing" e-mail by (a) allowing e-mail recipients to rank and comment on the content and relevance of e-mail messages and (b) providing better integration of e-mail with internal and external social media platforms. In addition, opportunities exist for e-mail technologies and information sharing technologies to have seamless integration points to enable users to easily tag and publish information from e-mail to more persistent and widely shared documents, wikis, blogs, and similar repositories.

The Most Important Three Steps to Consider

Putting in place clear guidelines and educational programs relating to the use of e-mail and social media in the workplace

The challenges related to the use of e-mail and social media are not going away anytime soon. On the contrary, they are mounting as adoptions of these platforms continue to grow exponentially. Creating clarity on what is expected and what constitutes inappropriate use is a necessary first step for companies to take. But just as importantly, companies need to supplement this with the necessary educational programs to establish awareness of the underlying issues and best practices, in an effort to help employees navigate through and manage these issues successfully.

Declaring social media as an important initiative and formalizing the social media effort

Having clear guidelines relating to the use of social media is a start, but the real benefits lie in harnessing social media's potential and directing its energy into useful applications. This effort can start by identifying the potential applications of social media and starting conversations about how to approach them. This is an area where leveraging internal knowledge can be key (as with Gen Y and Marketing professionals). Identifying selected applications, experimenting and gaining experience, and collecting real data are important first steps. The extent of the social media initiative needs to be proportional to the extent that the company customers, partners, and industry influencers are involved in social media. In addition, involving customers, partners, and industry influencers in this process can help steer these initiatives in the right direction.

Seeking improved tools and technologies that can help streamline the above effort

The use of tools and technologies currently seems to be very fragmented. Tools that can help streamline the use of e-mail and social media are still in their early development, and the adoption of the recently released applications (Jive Software, Telligent Systems Community Server, Cisco Quad, Salesforce.com Chatter, IBM Lotus Connections, Microsoft SharePoint Social Sites by NewsGator, Mzinga Social Media Suite, and many others) is still in the early stages. The process of starting to streamline the use of tools, working on optimizing integration points, and piloting some of the new technologies can help speed up this process and allow companies and employees to foster innovation and reap the benefits sooner rather than later.

Social Media and the Connected Leader

The Internet changed the world in the mid-90s. Social media changed it again a decade later and continues to do so in the current decade. Today's social media platforms, from Facebook to LinkedIn, Twitter, Google+, the blogosphere, and many others, offer extraordinary capabilities and unique opportunities, which can bring about significant business and personal benefits. However, many businesses and users are not necessarily realizing these benefits, either (a) getting caught up in the social media "chatter" and spending too much time in these platforms with little or no returns, (b) not fully leveraging the capabilities of these platforms, or (c) writing them off altogether as irrelevant or unimportant—the place where people post what they had for lunch.

The reality is that hundreds of millions of users are engaged in these platforms, and this large user base includes many if not most of your customers, employees, partners, colleagues, friends, and family members. As a leader, it is imperative to be "connected." This means understanding the social media challenges and opportunities we discussed earlier, becoming conversant in the key platforms, and leveraging them when relevant and appropriate. Social media business applications range from market research to recruiting, customer service, knowledge sharing, public relations, marketing and sales, fundraising, and more!

If you haven't ventured in the social media world yet, dismissing it as irrelevant or unimportant, the time has come for you to jump in. The approach I recommend consists of four stages: Learn, Listen, Experiment, and Influence. This is what we refer to as the Accomplishing More With Social Media Framework. The Learn stage consists of becoming familiar with the capabilities of these platforms by creating accounts and learning about what you can do in each. In Twitter for instance, this means learning about tweeting, replying, re-tweeting, using search, and using hash tags, among other things. In LinkedIn, this means creating your profile, using search and advanced search, and joining relevant groups. In Facebook, this would be learning about groups and pages. For blogs, this means becoming familiar with how blogs work and what makes blogs unique, including the ability to comment and subscribe.

Second comes the Listen phase. Who would you listen to? Here is a suggestion for a top ten list: Identify the top ten professionals in your industry, the top ten people in your company, the top ten people in your competition, the top ten authors that you enjoy, and the top ten colleagues and friends that you have common interests with. This is your top ten list, which consists of fifty connections. This is your starting point. Connect with them in the social media platforms and start to notice what topics they are posting about, what topics and people they are forwarding and replying to, and what value they are adding. You can also start to monitor what others are saying about your brand and your areas of interest.

Decide which platforms you're going to use for business purposes and which for personal use. For instance you might use Facebook to connect with family and friends, while you use LinkedIn and Twitter to connect with business contacts.

This brings you to the third phase, which is Experimenting. In this phase, you start to post information more often, reply to others and comment on articles, and continue to grow your network. Your top ten list is likely to grow to several hundred connections and a few dozen groups that are relevant to your field and areas of interest. You search often and find new and useful insights. You explore social media tools to help you manage your social media effort efficiently.

Finally comes the Influencer phase. Here, you are ready to identify your purpose more specifically and focus your social media effort on this purpose. Here is an example from a customer service professional:

My primary purpose	My secondary purpose	Not my purpose
Better serve our customers	Influence how people think about my company's brand	Directly market and sell my company's products

Another example from a career-minded professional:

My primary purpose	My secondary purpose	Not my purpose
Stay up-to-date on future trends in my field	Grow my network, and learn about who's who in my industry	Post trivial information, accumulate followers that have no relevance

As an influencer, you start to monitor the social media platforms and share information more regularly. You use social media tools to set up specific searches and monitor the results. You periodically engage in selected group discussions. Within your organization, you discuss the challenges and opportunities associated with the use of social media, and you promote best practices for using social media when applicable. You encourage the adoption of social media enterprise tools to help streamline the use of social media and to ensure measurable results. You encourage the use of internal social tools for internal communication and information sharing, including enterprise applications, wikis, and blogs.

Blogs are of particular importance when it comes to leveraging social media. Blogs have turned the publishing world upside down. They enabled readers to become publishers and publishers to become more connected with their readers. Not only can readers voice their comments on blogs, but they can also publish their own blogs. Creating a blog on a hosted blogging platform can be done in minutes, without any technical knowledge and with a minimum investment. Blogs can be used for business or personal use, and they can be private or public. A public business blog is an effective way to engage customers, partners, analysts and influencers, among others. A private business blog can be used to share knowledge internally and engage employees.

As an influencer, you identify your top ten blogs and subscribe to them. Use Google's blog search (blogsearch.google.com) to educate yourself about the blogs that are most relevant. Start to contribute comments and engage with the authors and readers. You also publish articles as a guest blogger or create your own blog.

Behaviors, behaviors, behaviors

Reflect on your job requirements, your functional area, and your industry, and identify the strengths that are required to succeed in this job. Reflect on your team and organization, and identify additional strengths that are required to succeed in this environment. Are you lacking any of these strengths? If so, you have uncovered a fatal flaw, and it is time to fix it. Work on a self-development plan. Consider having a coach or a mentor. Find someone who has these strengths with whom you can team up. Alternatively, you might consider seeking a new role, or adjusting your current role, so that it is a better fit for your strengths.

Get engaged with social media if you haven't yet, or if you have, then engage differently by incorporating the insights and techniques from this chapter. Identify your top ten list and connect with people on this list. Join the groups that are relevant. Use blogsearch.google.com to search for topics of interest and subscribe to these blogs. Listen to the conversations and contribute whenever you can add value. Define your purpose more specifically, and identify the ongoing social media activities that will enable you to fulfill this purpose.

Chapter 5: Navigating Personality and Leadership Styles

Personality Types

You are probably already familiar with one or more of the types of personal assessments that examine your preferences and style and then provide you with some indication of your personality type, along with a description of how your type explains certain preferences and behaviors that you have. Additionally, these assessments explain how certain careers are a better fit for you and why you have issues with certain people who happen to be of different types. Myers-Briggs Type Indicator (MBTI)[7] is one of these assessments. I chose it to illustrate personality types and their applications in business and leadership, mainly because of its popularity and the resources that are readily available if you choose to pursue further work in this area.

Regardless of which assessment or model you use, the key conclusions and their applications for leaders are similar. Once I discuss an abridged version of the MBTI, we will take a closer look at these applications. The MBTI examines four areas of our lives and assesses how we approach these areas.

The first area relates to how you get your energy. In this area, one can be an Extravert (E) or an Introvert (I). An Extravert is someone who tends to get their energy from socializing and interacting with the outside world, while an Introvert gets their energy from thinking and reflecting and having private time. In the actual assessment, you answer a series of questions, and, depending on your answers, your type in each area is then determined. In this abridged version, however, decide what you think your type is based on the description of each area. In this case, if you believe that your natural preference is one of an Extravert, jot down E as your type in this area, otherwise jot down I for Introvert.

Deciding your type may be challenging. You may think you are both an Extravert and an Introvert. You probably are. Most of us get energized from socializing and interacting with others at certain times but still can enjoy and use some alone time. The question, however, is which one is your preference and your default behavior.

---

[7] Refer to http://www.myersbriggs.org/ for more information about the Myers-Briggs Type Indicator®

It is likely that you have a preference towards one type, even if it is a slight preference. Ask yourself additional questions to uncover this preference. The last time you were leaving a party and one of your Extravert friends suggested going to the next party, how did you feel and what did you do? Did you seize the opportunity even though you were already exhausted and ready to retire? Or did you excuse yourself, preferring to end the night? Keep asking questions to uncover your preference.

The second area relates to how you absorb information and concepts. A Sensor (S) tends to prefer concrete information, step-by-step processes, and dealing with reality. An Intuitive (N), on the other hand, is big-picture oriented, likes to imagine concepts, and thinks about the future and all possibilities.

The third area has to do with how you make your decisions. A Thinker (T) is someone who makes decisions based on logic and prefers being objective. A Feeler (F) is someone who is more interested in the impact of these decisions on others and their aesthetic value. A Feeler is more subjective.

The fourth area has to do with how you approach life and take action. A Judger (J) is someone who likes to have a plan and who is very conscious of time. A Perceiver (P) is someone who goes with the flow, is flexible and opportunistic. Time is not of the essence for this type.

Jot down your type in each of these areas. You now have your four-letter MBTI personality type, such as ISTJ, ENFP, INTP, or any of the sixteen letter combinations which represent the sixteen types.

Personality Types Applications

As a leader, your stakeholders, including your team, are likely to be of a wide variety of personality types. Understanding personality types, yours and the people around you, helps you work with your stakeholders and lead your people and projects more effectively.

First, when hiring or forming teams, or assigning roles and responsibilities, this knowledge of personality types allows you to match people with the tasks for which they are more suited. Having a Perceiver in charge of the schedule, for instance, can be a recipe for frustration at best and for failure at worst. This may not be the case if the Perceiver was already aware of their type and its potential impact on the organization and has adopted some methods to stay on track and counteract the natural tendency to go with the flow. The matrices we discussed earlier (the Immediate Priorities Matrix and the End Results Matrix) are examples of such methods.

Second, being aware of personality types enables you to accept differences in working styles and manage these differences, instead of having them turn into destructive conflicts and become stumbling blocks. When the Sensor demands specific step-by-step instructions from an Intuitive, they are not doing so to annoy the Intuitive but, rather, to understand and be comfortable with the implementation plan. The Sensor may not realize that it would be helpful to explain the intention and purpose behind their questioning and may get quite upset with the reaction they get from the Intuitive. Add to that the fact that the Sensor may be an Extravert, demanding to discuss these steps verbally right now, while the Intuitive may be an Introvert and has already spent time putting this information in an e-mail that the Extravert has ignored. You get the idea! Educating your team about types can go a long way in helping them overcome such communication blunders.

Third, this knowledge of personality types allows you to be situational and potentially adapt your behavior depending on the person you are dealing with and the context you are in, instead of going along with your default behavior all the time. While your preference might be to go home after a company event, you may need to step up and approach one of your new team members and have a conversation to create rapport with them.

Ideally, a team would have a nice mix of personality types. Teams that are homogeneous are likely to have a "blind spot" and not necessarily produce the best outcome. A team of Introverts/Thinkers for instance, working with end-users or customers who are Extravert/Feelers, is likely to encounter communication hurdles. Having some Extraverts and Feelers on this team would help streamline the communication and resolve issues.

Leadership Styles

Similar to the personality types, there are numerous schools of thought on leadership styles. I chose the following styles[8] to help illustrate these concepts and provide some insights into the applications of styles.

Transactional Leadership Styles

This leader clarifies everyone's role and judges everyone based on their performance. According to this style, the employee is paid to do his or her job and the leader is paid to lead everyone. Some people thrive in this environment, but others find it too controlling and unsupportive of their development, which can lead to high turnover.

Autocratic Leadership Style

This is an extreme case of transactional leadership. This may work with routine and unskilled jobs. However, it is likely to cause people to be resentful and also lead to high turnover.

Bureaucratic Leadership Style

This style is characterized by imposing strict rules and procedures. This may be appropriate in certain fields where risk and security are critical. This is not likely to be effective where flexibility and creativity are needed.

Charismatic Leadership Style

This leader is inspiring and motivating. However, the charismatic leader doesn't necessarily grow and develop their organization. The organization may fall apart when the leader leaves.

Democratic/Participative Leadership Style

These leaders encourage participation and engage their team and organization, even though they still make the final decisions.

---

[8] Refer to http://www.mindtools.com/pages/article/newLDR_84.htm for more information about these styles.

This style is very motivating to people and is likely to produce better decisions and outcomes. On the other hand, this type of leader might take a long time to make decisions and act on them, and therefore this style may not work as well in fields and situations where speed and efficiency are critical for success.

Laissez-Faire Leadership Style

This leader gives the team the freedom to make decisions and act on their own. The leader gives support by providing resources and input. This style can work well when team members are experienced and skilled. It is very motivating and fulfilling and can lead to great outcomes. It may not work as well in situations where risk and security are critical or where process is necessary to guide a less skilled workforce.

Task-Oriented Leadership Style

The focus in this style is to get the job done. It is likely to involve defining clear roles and managing people's performance. It resembles the transactional and autocratic style, but it is more focused on results.

People-Oriented/Relations-Oriented Leadership Style

The focus in this style is on supporting and developing people, as well as encouraging teamwork and collaboration—the opposite of task-oriented style. This style enables people to take risks and potentially achieve breakthroughs that may not otherwise be possible. However, if overdone, it is possible that tasks and performance become secondary, which can therefore jeopardize the overall success of the organization.

Servant Leadership Style

The emphasis in this style is on meeting the needs of the people in the organization. This style is more suited for politics or in positions where the leader is elected to serve in their position. This style may not work well in competitive situations.

Transformational Leadership Style

This leader inspires people with a shared vision, sets clear goals, and motivates people to meet these goals. This leader communicates well with their organization and is attentive to the needs of the people. This style, however, requires the support of transactional managers who can take care of the implementation details.

Leadership Styles Applications

Now what? What do we do with this knowledge of leadership styles? First and foremost, this knowledge presents an opportunity for you to reflect on your leadership style and consider making adjustments if and when necessary. Is your style appropriate for your work environment, and is it bringing about the results that you are after? How are the people around you responding to your style? Are you finding situations where your style is not necessarily working? Would you benefit from adopting a different style or adapting your style in certain situations?

Adopting a different style or adapting your style depending on the situation requires not only awareness of styles but also a broad and flexible behavioral repertoire. To develop such a repertoire, you need to have the willingness to challenge your comfort zone and experiment with new ways of thinking and behaving! Behaviors, behaviors, behaviors. This is the main theme in our leadership journey.

The road to happiness and fulfillment

Earlier in the book, I introduced the concept of a sweet spot as being the area of your work where you are strong and that you are passionate about. I also posed some reflection questions. The first focused on what you would do to expand your sweet spot and therefore be happier and more fulfilled. Similarly, how would you help your team members experience this feeling and reap the rewards? Finally, what would you do if this sweet spot were non-existent, which translates into work being difficult and not so rewarding?

If you find yourself or a team member in this situation, consider the same recommendations that we discussed when handling a fatal flaw. This translates into informal and formal learning to expand your circle of strengths, which will help you start to enjoy these areas as you grow and develop. This also translates into negotiating your role and responsibilities to exclude these areas and include more of your strengths and areas that you enjoy. The road to fulfillment and happiness starts with awareness of these issues and ends with persistent growth and adjustments through effective negotiation, a topic that we will embark on very soon.

Behaviors that take no time

In almost every conversation with our leadership program participants, we hear them express that they don't have time! To help them break out of this vicious cycle of not having time and therefore not being able to practice the leadership behaviors that will help them save time, we came up with a list of ten behaviors that take little or no time but have a big impact. These behaviors make time.

First: Focus for thirty minutes

Focus doesn't take time. Focus makes time. In a thirty-minute focused session, you accomplish what would otherwise take two hours. Just as importantly, at the end of your focused session, you feel accomplished instead of overwhelmed and therefore energized instead of exhausted.

Second: Micro-Planning

It only takes a minute or two to prepare a Micro-Plan for an important and involved task. The Micro-Plan, however, gives you a clear purpose and keeps you on track. It helps you to more easily and quickly recover from interruptions and therefore creates time.

Third: Use a timer

It takes no time to set a timer. Upon starting your focused session, set that timer and enjoy a heightened awareness of time. The timer retrains your brain to be less scattered and to wander off less often, again creating substantial time for you.

Fourth: Work in bursts

After intense focus, engage in intense collaboration, and then intense or relaxed play. This method of working is highly efficient and energizing and therefore saves you time while enabling you to accomplish more.

Fifth: Stop and breathe

The breathing exercise I described earlier takes just a few minutes. Our workshop participants persistently report feeling more relaxed and having a clearer mind even after three minutes of the breathing exercise. It only takes three minutes to change your physical and mental state and be ready to take on the next challenge.

Sixth: Stop and stretch

Similarly, a few minutes of stretching increase the blood flow through the body and relax the muscles that otherwise get tight due to physical and mental stress. Relaxing tight muscles can undo the emotions that created the tightness in the first place.

Seventh: Prepare your Immediate Priorities Matrix

While the Immediate Priorities Matrix takes fifteen to twenty minutes to prepare, it helps you reshape the next week or two, saving you substantial worry and considerable time. Blocking time on your calendar for your priorities, setting expectations, and negotiating are vital for creating some sanity in today's hectic work environment.

Eight: Start your day with the journal

Before you dive into e-mail, calendar, to-do lists and the like, take a few minutes to allow your intuition to guide you into identifying what is important and what you intend to accomplish today. These few minutes are likely to shape your day and turn it into a great success.

Nine: Acknowledging your own strengths

Your strengths are with you at all times. It takes little time to become more aware of them and take every opportunity to leverage them. When you leverage your strengths, you are efficient and are saving time.

Ten: Give praise

Similarly, it takes little time to notice other people's strengths and acknowledge them. The impact on the working relationship and on their self-confidence is substantial. It is also currency that you can use later when things get tough.

Behaviors, Behaviors, Behaviors

Reflect on your personality type and leadership style and identify opportunities where you can behave "situationally" to achieve greater outcomes. Take this to the next level by experimenting with style-switching for a day. If you happen to be an Extravert, for instance, behave like an Introvert. Seek some reflective time instead of socializing. Stop every so often and journal about your experience, instead of talking about it to others. If you happen to be an Introvert, think out loud and volunteer information instead of listening, even when your thoughts are not polished.

Schedule a day or half-day in which you turn off e-mail and work on important and strategic tasks. The world will continue to revolve even if you are not on e-mail. If anything, the world will revolve more smoothly because you are likely to think and act strategically and creatively, thus contributing more fully to whatever endeavor you undertake during this time. Here are some suggestions to make this experience unique and effective:

1. Set expectations ahead of time that you won't be available, and, if necessary, find someone who can cover for you during this time.

2. Be somewhere that is comfortable and conducive to creativity and away from interruptions and noise.

3. Have an overall plan for what you want to accomplish.

4. Divide this time into small chunks of fifteen to thirty minutes.

5. Prepare a Micro-Plan at the beginning of each chunk.

6. Stop in between these bursts of focused time to reflect on what you accomplished, and acknowledge your accomplishments no matter how small you think they are.

7. Don't forget to play. Stretch, walk, do the breathing exercise, listen to music, and journal.

Consider giving someone on your team the opportunity to do the same. Consider repeating this and maybe making it a weekly or monthly routine!

Chapter 6: Mastering Negotiating, Problem Solving, and Decision Making

The "What worked, what didn't, and now what" Practice

What worked

Jot down something that you did well recently, small or big. Maybe you focused for thirty minutes on an important task, you took the opportunity to praise someone, you resolved a team conflict productively, or you had a successful customer presentation. Give yourself a pat on the back, and I mean literally let your right arm reach behind your left shoulder, and give yourself a pat on the back.

What didn't work

Jot down something that you didn't work so well recently. Maybe you overreacted to someone's opinion or behavior, you procrastinated on an important task and missed the deadline, or you deviated from you diet or exercise plan. Give yourself a pat on the back for acknowledging this.

Now what!

Next, move to the "now what"! Jot down ideas for the next actions, and, if applicable, block some time on your calendar to follow up and plan or take these actions. Give yourself a third pat on the back for doing this.

Practice this formula often so it becomes second nature. Practice it with your team so it becomes everyone's second nature.

Negotiation Styles

Thomas Kilmann's[9] instrument remains one of the most meaningful explanations of negotiation styles. According to this instrument, styles are assessed based on two measurements. One relates to how assertive one's style is, and the other relates to how cooperative it is. As a result, the following styles emerge, which are also shown in the chart below:

---

[9]http://www.kilmanndiagnostics.com/catalog/thomas-kilmann-conflict-mode-instrument

Competing: This describes someone who is very assertive but not cooperative. Their goal is to win without much consideration to the other party's interests.

Accommodating: This is the opposite of competing, which translates into not assertive at all and overly cooperative. Their goal is to yield without much consideration to their own interests.

Avoiding: This describes someone who is not assertive and not cooperative. Their goal is to postpone and not face the issues, even if this at the detriment of the interests of both parties.

Compromising: This describes someone who is somehow assertive and cooperative. Their goal is to get to an agreement. They seek compromises from both parties in order to do so.

Collaborating: This describes someone who is very assertive and very cooperative. Their goal is to reach an agreement that satisfies the interest of both parties.

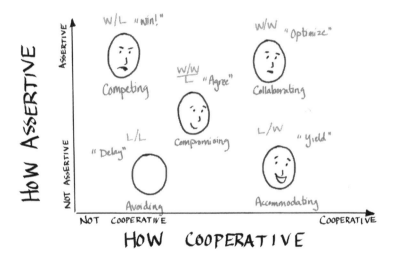

Which is your primary style? Do you consistently use this style or do you sometimes resort to other styles and under what circumstances? What are the styles of the people on your team and others that you interact with?

Being aware of your own negotiation style and that of others helps you adapt your style based on the situation and on the style of the people with whom you are negotiating. While the Collaborative style is the most desirable, especially when the issues at hand are considerably important, there are situations where other styles may prove to be effective. The Competing style can be useful when you need to protect yourself against people who take advantage of non-competitive styles. Compromising may be appropriate when the goal is not important enough to justify the effort or political currency that you would otherwise spend. Avoiding can be used when the issue is trivial, when others can resolve it better, or to let people calm down before starting the negotiation process. Even the Accommodating style has some uses, such as when preserving harmony is more important than the potential benefits.

Negotiation Matrix

Regardless of the styles, the core of the negotiation is still about the issues. Being prepared to discuss and negotiate the core issues is vital. The AMLP Negotiation Matrix from our leadership program helps you research and think through the issues at hand and be ready to optimize the outcome of your negotiation:

Table 1: AMLP[10] Negotiation Matrix

Your Needs[11]:	Their Needs (to the best of your knowledge):
Your Assets:	Their Assets:

---

[10] AMLP refers to the Accomplishing More Leadership Program
http://www.people-onthego.com/accomplishing-more-leadership-program
[11] Needs include motivation, objectives, and interests

Your additional parameters to consider:	**Their additional parameters to consider:**
Your potential concessions/incentives to the other party (to them):	**Their potential concessions/incentives to the other party (to you):**
Your BATNA[12]:	**Their BATNA:**

Preparing for negotiation

Underlying the Negotiation Matrix are three important elements to keep in mind:

Knowledge: The more you know, the better off you are during the negotiation process. Spend some time researching and collecting relevant information.

Relationships: The better the relationship you have with the other party, the more successful the negotiation is likely to

---

[12] BATNA refers to Best Alternative To a Negotiated Agreement

be. Build or rebuild the relationships ahead of time, whenever possible.

Rehearsal: If you can anticipate some of the arguments or objections they are likely to bring up, script your responses and practice them. Even if you don't use your scripted responses, you will feel confident and able to think more clearly and handle the unexpected.

Problem Solving Matrix

Leaders solve problems and coach others to become problem solvers. Leaders also recognize that not all problems are worth the effort of solving. As depicted in the chart below, your effort is best spent on the problems that fall in the top right quadrant, which we refer to as quadrant 1. The problems in this quadrant are significant, and you have some degree of influence over them:

When it comes to the other quadrants, here are some strategies to consider.

Quadrant 2 (top left): This is where important problems lie but where you have little influence to solve them. You have three essential choices when it comes to such problems. One is to simply accept the situation, along with the related side effects, and move on to other more fruitful endeavors. Another is to negotiate and try to reach a suitable arrangement that would address the situation. The third is to confront the situation and demand an agreeable solution. Whichever approach you take, it is important to keep in mind that this quadrant is not necessarily the best place to invest your time and energy.

Quadrant 3 (bottom left): This quadrant is not for leaders. Once leaders determine that the problem lies in this quadrant, they move on and don't let such problems take any emotional or mental space.

Quadrant 4 (bottom right): While this has similarities to quadrant 1, in that you have some degree of influence here, it is also not a great investment of your time. Either solve the problem quickly or leave it alone and move on. This quadrant can be deceiving for many. Spending time in this quadrant gives one the false impression of control and of making progress. However, knowing that the problems in this quadrant are not related to the core results, the overall output is minuscule and the impact on the results is negligible, while the opportunity cost incurred is huge.

Once you identify a problem in quadrant 1, or maybe a problem in quadrant 2 that you would like to address, it is time to engage in problem solving in a new way. The AMLP Problem Solving Matrix below helps you break the problem into manageable components and then apply the most appropriate problem-solving strategy for each component.

Table 2: AMLP Problem Solving Matrix

Component	Strategy	Brainstorming	Best option	Action

The strategies are similar to those we discussed earlier: Address, accept, negotiate, or confront. The brainstorming follows. Brainstorming involves thinking through the core issues and coming up with options. This might involve research and data gathering, as well as consulting with others. Once some options are identified, then you determine the best option and create an action plan.

Decision making models

There is a crucial leadership question that needs to be asked before any decision making begins. What is this question? The crucial leadership question is: Does this relate to a Delta or a Weak Link? If a Weak Link, then make the decision quickly or delegate it to the person who is closest to the issue or who has the most relevant strengths. Don't get caught in the Weak Link decisions, and don't allow your team to get caught in them either. This needs to be non-negotiable!

If the decision relates to a Delta, then identify the appropriate approach for the decision. Based on the Vroom-Yetton model[13], here are the potential approaches.

Autocratic I: Leader makes decision on her own.

Autocratic II: Leader asks for information from followers, one at a time. Then leader makes decision on his own. Follower involvement is limited to providing information.

Consultative I: Leader presents problem to followers, one at a time, and asks for suggestions. Then leader makes decision on his own.

Consultative II: Leader presents problem to followers as a group and asks for suggestions but still makes decision on her own.

Group: Leader presents problem to followers and brainstorms with the group, coming up with a decision that is acceptable to the group.

To help you decide which approach to take, the Vroom-Yetton model suggests a series of questions and provides the chart shown below to guide you through the process of identifying the approach that is most appropriate for your decision:

1. Is there a quality requirement? Is the nature of the solution critical? Are there technical or rational grounds for selecting among possible solutions?

2. Do I have sufficient information to make a high-quality decision?

3. Is the problem structured? Are the alternative courses of action and methods for their evaluation known?

4. Is acceptance of the decision by subordinates critical to its implementation?

---

[13] The Vroom-Yetton model is a situational leadership theory or industrial and organizational psychology developed by Victor Vroom in collaboration with Philip Yetton (1973) and later with Jago (1988).

5. If I were to make the decision by myself, is it reasonably certain that my subordinates would accept it?

6. Do subordinates share the organizational goals to be obtained in solving this problem?

7. Is conflict among subordinates likely in obtaining the preferred solution?

Table 3: Vroom-Yetton decision-making chart

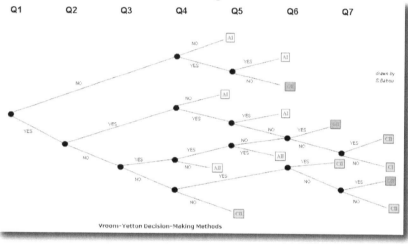

Vroom-Yetton Decision-Making Methods

Overall, and regardless of the approach, the decision-making process is most effective when it involves the following steps, especially when the decision is significant and has a big impact on the people and the business:

1. Definition: Defining the issue clearly and specifying the parameters surrounding the issue.

2. Research and understanding: Researching the facts, gathering the stakeholders' views and opinions, understanding their feelings, and considering their needs and wants.

3. Exploration: Exploring options, weighing pros and cons, costs and benefits, and related risks.

4. Selection: Selecting the best option.

5. Testing: Testing key elements of the selected option, especially any underlying assumptions.

6. Finalizing: Finalizing the decision and the implementation plan, including key milestones when applicable.

7. Follow-through: Is the implementation plan unfolding as envisioned? What are we learning along the way? What adjustments need to happen to enhance or remedy the situation?

Speed Matters

In the previous chapter, I outlined ten behaviors that take no time and that can help you become more effective and more fulfilled! How about things that take time? This is where the concept of speed comes into play. I alluded to this concept very early on, and it is time to explore it in more detail and discover the five dimensions to speed.

Physical speed: This is the most obvious dimension and it involves moving faster from point A to point B, whatever the context is. In today's knowledge work, this is the least significant dimension, but it still has some merits and can be energizing. This might include walking a bit faster, organizing and filing papers faster, or even typing faster.

Mental speed: This is where breakthroughs happen. Mental speed is specifically about focus. It is engaging in intense focus to get the task at hand done in twenty minutes instead of spending two hours working on the same task a few minutes here and a few minutes there. Mental speed is exhilarating. It is a mental ride. When you approach your task with the mindset that there is no way out, just like a ride, and accept the inherent ups and downs and keep at it until the time is up, you discover some amazing accomplishments and a new you! The Results Curve and the working in bursts behaviors are at the core of mental speed.

Strategic speed: This is about focusing on the Deltas and minimizing the time and energy spent on Weak Links. As we illustrated earlier, when focusing on the Deltas, you get 40 percent more results without investing any time at all. Imagine the possibilities.

Emotional speed: With emotional speed, instead of dwelling on problems and issues and getting stuck in your thoughts and feelings, you explore these thoughts and feelings methodically and move into examining your needs and wants and the potential actions that will get you the desired outcome. Soon, I will be introducing the Awareness Wheel technique, which will help achieve emotional speed.

Psychological speed: Psychological speed goes one level deeper. It is about facing the fear. It consists of identifying the thoughts behind your deep-seated fears and shattering them, replacing these thoughts with more realistic and constructive ones, therefore eradicating these fears and moving towards accomplishment and happiness at a speed you never experienced before. We will explore this dimension later in the book.

The paradox is that if you practice speed the way I outlined it above, not only will you find more time and get more accomplished, but you will also feel calmer and discover a sense of peacefulness.

Behaviors, Behaviors, Behaviors

The next time you have an issue to negotiate, prepare the AMLP Negotiation Matrix ahead of time and use it to guide you through the negotiation process. Instead of using your usual negotiation style, consider adapting your style depending on the issue at hand and the style of the other party.

When you are faced with an important problem or challenge, prepare the AMLP Problem Solving Matrix to help you think through the problem methodically, explore options, and identify next steps.

When you have an important decision to make, determine the approach that is most suitable for this decision. Involve others as necessary and follow the steps that I outlined above to reach an effective decision and an applicable implementation plan.

Practice being situational. Identify at least one opportunity every day when you can change your behavior based on the situation and the people involved. Being situational can apply to your personality type, your leadership style, and your negotiation style, among other areas. Reflect upon the situation ahead of time, if possible. When the opportunity comes up, try the different behavior.

Remember to give yourself a pat on the back, regardless of how well you executed.

Cancel a Weak Link meeting this week and just "disappear" and do something fun. It is a Weak Link anyway! You will find it freeing and energizing to replace such a meeting with something invigorating. You will be surprised to find out that your total output on that day is likely to be greater. Dare to cancel Weak Link meetings more often and replace them by Delta activities!

Chapter 7: Cultivating Awareness and Creating Learning Communities

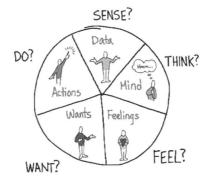

More about negotiation

One important aspect of negotiation that we touched upon earlier, and which I would like to emphasize again, is having data to support you through the negotiation process. This makes the Immediate Priorities Matrix and the End Results Matrix powerful negotiation tools. Having the Immediate Priorities Matrix, for instance, positions you as a problem solver and a win-win player, not only when you want to negotiate with your stakeholders but also with your team when the members come to you with problems. Help them prepare their Immediate Priorities Matrix on the spot, and work with them on prioritizing and addressing bottlenecks and resource conflicts. Moving forward, instead of them coming to you with problems, ask them to come to you with the matrix and with options and recommendations!

Chocolate Tasting

You will need to find some dark chocolate to participate in this experiential exercise. Place a piece of dark chocolate in your hand and observe its shape, edges, and texture. Turn it around and continue to observe. Close your eyes and smell it. Is the smell unique? What does it remind you of? With your eyes closed, put it in your mouth but don't chew on it yet. Let it melt slowly as you enjoy the taste. When you are ready, start to chew it slowly as you continue to notice the changes in the taste and aftertaste.

What was this exercise about? This exercise was mainly about paying attention. This is what I also refer to as being present. Being present is not mysterious, as it is sometimes conveyed to be. It is simply paying attention to what is going on around us. It involves focusing on where we are, as opposed to getting lost in our imaginary thoughts and losing touch with reality!

This exercise is also about engaging our senses more fully, in order to have a richer and more memorable experience. Lastly, this exercise is about enjoying dark chocolate, which happens to have many health benefits—of course when consumed in reasonable quantities.

The Awareness Wheel

The Awareness Wheel, a technique that was originally described by Sherod and Phyllis Miller, authors of *Core Communication: Skills and Processes*, can help us take a difficult situation, break it down into more manageable components, and identify how best to handle it. The prerequisite to using the Awareness Wheel is to clearly define the situation or issue at hand. Clearly defining the situation is an important first step in this process. When the situation is not clearly defined, it is difficult to work through it. It would be like chasing a ghost.

The next step is to break down this seemingly difficult situation into five components, which are represented by five sections of the wheel:

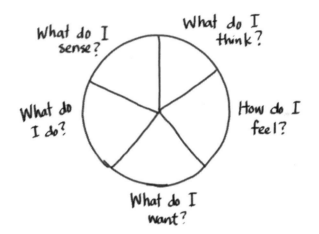

Each component presents a question that you need to answer to the best of your knowledge. These questions prompt us to think more thoroughly about the situation and identify what is truly going on, so we can be in a better position to manage the situation. Here are the questions:

1. *What do I sense about the situation?* We have five senses that give us factual data about our environment. The point

here is to identify what this data is, such as what we saw and what we heard.

2. *What do I think about the situation?* This has to do with what is going on in our mind. This ranges from interpretations to opinions, conclusions, and the myriad of other thoughts that go through our mind.

3. *How do I feel about the situation?* On one side of the spectrum of feelings may be anger and fear, and on the other side of the spectrum may be extreme joy and happiness. And of course, there are all shades in between.

4. *What do I want in this situation?* This has to do with reflecting on what we want as opposed to staying in reaction mode and being sidetracked by our thoughts and feelings.

5. *What do I do in this situation?* This has to do with identifying the potential actions that can help resolve the situation and, ideally, the best possible action.

In a perfect world, we would be able to run through these questions one by one, become more aware of what is really going on, and be in a better position to identify and take the appropriate action. In the real world however, as a result of the complexity of the human mind and emotions and the interdependence between thoughts and feelings, we are likely to go through these questions multiple times (hence, the concept of a wheel) and not necessarily in order. The case study below illustrates how the Awareness Wheel can be applied to help better manage a difficult situation.

The case study

Mark is unhappy at work. When asked to define the problem, here is how he put it: "My boss doesn't care about my professional development, and I am really unhappy at work." This situation is very stressful for Mark and is taking up a lot of his energy. His working relationships are impacted, he is not feeling good at work or even outside of work, and his performance is suffering. Let us see how the Awareness Wheel can help. We will demonstrate how a coach can help Mark use the Awareness Wheel to manage this situation:

Coach: "Mark, what happened?"

Mark: "She doesn't care."

Where does Mark's statement ("She doesn't care.") fall in the Awareness Wheel? This is Mark's subjective view of what happened. This is clearly his interpretation of what happened. It is a thought. The coach makes a note of this in the Awareness Wheel, indicating to Mark that this is his interpretation, and repeats the question again:

Coach: "Tell me more about what actually happened."

Mark: "She cancelled the meeting."

This is a fact. Mark reports real data. He *saw* the meeting cancellation notice in his e-mail inbox. The coach makes note of this and proceeds to help Mark explore the feeling part:

Coach: "Mark, how do you feel about the meeting being cancelled?"

Mark: "I feel I am not important."

Even though Mark uses the words "I feel," the statement "I am not important" is more of an interpretation than a feeling. Using words such as "I feel" to express a thought is common. There might be a feeling associated with the thought, but that is something that would need to be explored. For now, the "I am not important" statement is noted as a thought. Now the coach tries to get to the feeling behind the thought:

Coach: "Mark, how else are you feeling about this?"

Mark pauses for a bit and then says: "I am sad and disappointed."

As you may have noticed already, the coach tends to repeat the questions to get to the real answers. The first answer is usually a reactionary answer, such as "I feel that I am not important," and then the second answer (or sometimes the third or fourth) is more meaningful and insightful, such as "I am sad and disappointed."

The coach continues to explore this area with Mark, and then when he thinks that Mark is ready to move to the next component, the coach makes an initial attempt at asking Mark about his wants:

Coach: "So what do you want Mark?"

Mark: "I want to have the meeting."

Then Mark proceeds to say: "I will tell her that I am unhappy."

Mark has just expressed an action here (not necessarily the best action, but it is an action). The coach notices that the want and action expressed by Mark are reactionary, so he asks Mark again about his thoughts and feelings regarding the situation and gives him the opportunity to express these further and spend time exploring them. Then later in the conversation, the coach makes another attempt at asking Mark about what Mark wants:

Mark takes a deep breath at that point and says: "I want more recognition."

Then Mark adds: "I want input on my career development."

This is a big aha moment for Mark! Mark just realized it is not the meeting that really got him upset and stressed; it is the underlying need to feel recognized and the desire for a better career development plan. The meeting was just the tip of the iceberg, and his reaction to the meeting being cancelled is just that, a reaction. This is one of the key purposes of the wheel—to facilitate the process of becoming more aware of the real causes behind what we are experiencing on the surface.

Occasionally, our leadership program participants indicate that Mark should have easily realized it was not the meeting that was causing his stress ("What is the big deal about a meeting being cancelled anyway?") and that it should have been clear to him the lack of recognition and lack of career development opportunities were the real issues. When someone on my team or I talk to these participants further about the issues that are causing them stress, we find out that their issues are not more severe or different in nature from Mark's issues, and yet, these participants seem to get significantly stressed and emotionally involved when it comes to their own issues. So how does it happen that we have more clarity when it comes to other people's issues but suddenly lose this clarity when it comes to our own issues?

This is largely because when we are experiencing the issues ourselves, we are "under the influence" of our emotions, and therefore our judgment gets somehow impaired. At this point, when our judgment is impaired, even the smartest of us become unable to make the distinction between facts, thoughts, and feelings. Our emotions and deep-seated fears take over. So while Mark's situation may seem easy for someone looking at it from the outside—maybe someone who hasn't experienced a similar situation—it doesn't look that way to Mark and probably not to anyone who has experienced a similar situation.

In order to truly experience the Awareness Wheel, to better understand it and see its usefulness, you need to apply it to a real situation that is causing you confusion and stress.

Coming back to the conversation with Mark, the coach is now ready to ask the important question:

Coach: "So what are you going to do about this situation Mark?"

Mark: "I will ask to reschedule the meeting and discuss the real issues with my boss."

Then Mark adds: "I will also find a coach or a mentor."

Another big aha!

The Awareness Wheel helped transform this difficult situation (or even seemingly insurmountable situation, in Mark's mind at the time) into an actionable one. We started with "My boss doesn't care about my professional development, and I am really unhappy at work" and ended up with a better understanding of the underlying needs and specific action items that can be carried out in order to get these underlying needs met. Nicely done!

The job is not done, however. Mark still needs to implement these actions. As he implements the actions, he needs to watch for his interpretations and assumptions sneaking in again. If he continues practicing the Awareness Wheel each step of the way, he will continue to refine and enhance his actions. Soon he will become experienced at this tool and use it more often to help him through difficult situations. He is now on his way to discovering a whole new world of accomplishments.

The purpose of the wheel

To start with, the simple act of defining the "issue" and getting engaged with the Awareness Wheel is in and of itself an empowering exercise. It puts our energy and creativity in motion. It helps us challenge the status quo and get busy with solutions—all essential to solving problems and feeling better. In addition, the Awareness Wheel serves several important and clear purposes:

1. It helps us separate reality from imagination, facts from interpretations.

2. It helps us separate thoughts from feelings (what the mind is creating, as opposed to how we are truly feeling).

3. It helps us identify our true wants (instead of our reactionary wants).

4. It facilitates identifying the best possible action.

5. It enables us to positively influence the end results.

In our daily work and personal lives, an event takes place in our environment, we quickly interpret it in a certain way, which invokes certain feelings, and then we act accordingly. This may lead to poor actions based on interpretations and assumptions that are not realistic. This sequence of events/interpretations/feelings/actions happens very quickly and transparently. We don't even notice it. It looks and feels as if we are just taking actions to deal with what happened, and we wonder why we aren't getting the results we desire. The Awareness Wheel enables us to intervene and change this sequence. The end goal is to have significantly improved actions and results, not to mention make breakthroughs!

So what if there is nothing we can do about the situation?

What if we go through the Awareness Wheel, exhaust our creative thinking and problem solving capabilities, and still conclude that there isn't much that we can do about the situation? If this is the case, it would be beneficial for us to stop banging our head against this situation and move on to better things, where our effort is fruitful and rewarding. The Awareness Wheel helps us make that determination faster and reach the acceptance stage sooner. I would even suggest, once we reach the acceptance stage, creating a "closed issues" list and adding the issue to this list, so that your mind doesn't keep resurrecting the "closed" issue and wasting valuable energy.

Self-Coaching

We presented the case study above by having a coach walk through the Awareness Wheel with Mark. While it would be ideal to have a coach help us along the way, more often than not, we need to be our own coach. The Awareness Wheel is the ideal tool for self-coaching.

The Awareness Wheel components and related questions are exactly the kind of questions we should ask ourselves. Writing down the answers, as we progress through the process, is critical. This helps us avoid "spinning our wheels" by reiterating the same thoughts and feelings endlessly. This will also help us detect *imbalance* (spending too much time and energy on one component of the wheel without paying enough attention to the rest). The Awareness Wheel is largely about balance. It helps bring to the forefront all aspects of a situation. It helps us have a more objective view of the world, as opposed to getting too focused on one area and losing ourselves in it.

As we saw in the case study, it is important to repeat the same question more than once to get beyond the initial reaction and superficial answers. It usually takes several passes through the wheel to get to the underlying issues. If you don't get to the desired results in one session, give yourself a break and let the issues percolate for a day or two before you resume your effort. This process of self-questioning and self-coaching is the foundation for becoming an aware and effective leader.

Coaching others

When it comes to coaching others using the Awareness Wheel, there are more things to consider. If you are in the midst of a conflict-ridden situation or a heated discussion with the other person, while it is tempting to introduce the Awareness Wheel, your good intentions may not generate the desired results, as the other person may not be open to your coaching in this moment. However, if you have already built trust with the other person and introduced the Awareness Wheel ahead of time, and if you both agree that it would be beneficial, things can be much more promising.

In situations where it is not possible or appropriate to share the Awareness Wheel and coach each other, one can still keep the Awareness Wheel in mind and apply the techniques naturally, to help address the situation. Using the Awareness Wheel should not depend on the other party and does not need to be a formal exercise. It can help us better understand what is going on for us and potentially for the other party, and both people can have a more effective interaction as a result.

Clear communication and more

In addition to being an ideal tool for coaching, the Awareness Wheel is a vehicle for clear and effective communication at large.

For instance, instead of uttering "I can't believe you canceled this meeting at this stage in the project," you might say "I saw that this meeting was cancelled" (the senses) and "My interpretation is that this issue is not seen as important right now" (the thought expressed in a non-threatening way, acknowledging that this is your interpretation and you are open to the possibility of having misinterpreted the fact) and "I am concerned" (feeling). You might add "I would like to explore how we can move this issue forward and not run into potential project delays later" (want) and then conclude with "I am wondering if you have some input on how we can address this?" (request for action in the form of a question and also an attempt at soliciting their help). This is mature communication that can be achieved by practicing the Awareness Wheel and applying it genuinely in everyday situations. There are no tricks here. This is authentic expression of what is going on, stated so to achieve effective resolutions to the underlying issues and a win-win outcome.

Another example might be as follows: Instead of starting your meeting with "Here is our agenda: I am unhappy about the delays we are experiencing. Let us dive into this topic right away," you might start with "I need your help today in making this meeting highly effective and focused on the core challenges that we are facing" (wants and facts), "I am concerned about the delays we are experiencing" (feeling), and "I believe that if we put our heads together and think through these issues creatively, we will be able to get back on track and feel good about this project" (more thoughts and feelings but mainly a hint to an important want, which is getting back on track). In addition, you might add "Let us examine the facts first, get your thoughts and impressions, and brainstorm on some options" (senses, thoughts, feelings, and paving the road to actions).

As you see in the examples above, instead of communicating interpretations and assumptions as if they were facts and jumping into action while ignoring everything in between, you are enabled by the Awareness Wheel to consider the full spectrum, from facts to thoughts, feelings, and wants, therefore paving the road to effective action. Invite others to do the same. This applies whether you are communicating a simple issue to someone or discussing a complex situation with your team or whole department.

The Awareness Wheel is also about being present, instead of getting lost in the past or future and feeling dissatisfied and unproductive in the present as a result. Instead of spending precious moments and consuming valuable energy reliving unpleasant past experiences or feeling stressed and overwhelmed by imagined future situations, the Awareness Wheel helps you acknowledge your thoughts and feelings about these situations and brings you back to noticing what is going on around you now, prompting you to reflect on what you want and redirecting you to action when applicable. This is healthy and happy living. This is also proactive stress management. Finally, during negotiation, problem solving, and decision making, use the wheel to help uncover underlying interpretations and assumptions and create clarity, understanding, rapport, and enhanced outcomes.

Emotional Speed

Speed matters. As discussed earlier, speed has several dimensions including physical, mental, strategic, emotional, and psychological. The Awareness Wheel is our method for achieving emotional speed. Instead of dwelling on and getting lost in our thoughts and feelings, the wheel prompts us to consider our facts, our wants, and our actions, thus freeing us to move forward constructively. Mark, in our case study above, could have spent days or weeks consumed by his thoughts and feelings. The wheel helped him get to the underlying issues, become aware of what was going on, and then move into an effective action.

The fixed and growth mindset

Carol Dweck, Ph.D., is a Stanford professor who spent years researching why some people fulfill their potential and why some don't. Her findings point out that when people believe that their basic traits are fixed, which she refers to as "fixed mindset," they limit themselves and create obstacles that stand in the way of their success and happiness. On the other hand, when people believe that their qualities are things that they can develop, which she refers to as "growth mindset," they learn and achieve and pave the road to fulfillment.

In her book *Mindset: The New Psychology of Success*[14], Dr. Dweck provides a simple assessment to help determine if one has a fixed or growth mindset by asking which of these statements you mostly agree with:

1. Your intelligence is something basic about you that you can't change very much

---

[14] Carol Dweck, Ph.D., *Mindset: The New Psychology of Success* (New York: Random House, 2006)

2. You can learn new things, but you can't really change how intelligent you are

3. No matter how much intelligence you have, you can always change it quite a bit

4. You can always substantially change how intelligent you are

Statements 1 and 2 indicate a fixed mindset, while statements 3 and 4 indicate a growth mindset. It is possible to display both mindsets, but most people lean towards one or the other. You could also substitute "artistic talent," "sports ability," or "business skill," for "intelligence" in the above statements and assess your mindset in these areas.

It is not only your abilities; it is also your personal qualities that can be in question. Dr. Dweck proceeds to provide yet another assessment related to personal qualities by asking with which of these statements do you mostly agree:

1. You are a certain kind of person, and there is not much that can be done to change that

2. No matter what kind of person you are, you can always change substantially

3. You can do things differently, but the important parts of who you are can't really be changed.

4. You can always change basic things about the kind of person you are

Statements 1 and 3 reflect the fixed mindset statements; 2 and 4 reflect the growth mindset. Which statement did you agree with? Does your mindset here differ from your intelligent mindset?

Beware, however. It is tempting to quickly conclude that you have a growth mindset. The real test is not our perception of our mindset but our behaviors and the impact we have on our surroundings. Here are a few more questions that I suggest you consider:

1. When was the last time you felt stressed and overwhelmed, and how did you deal with the situation? Did you feel threatened, helpless, and/or impatient? Or did you soon

confront the situation and work your way through it, in spite of the uncertainty and discomfort?

2. When was the last time you felt defensive? And how far did you go in defending yourself? Or did you acknowledge your part in the situation and move into resolving it constructively?

3. When was the last time you reflected closely on how others perceive you and paid attention to the impact you have on others? Did you seek feedback from others or did you ignore any signs of trouble or even justify them?

4. When was the last time you took on a new initiative, activity, or task that was not necessarily easy and didn't essentially match your natural strengths? Did you challenge the status quo and venture into expanding your horizon? Or did you stick to what you know and what you are good at?

5. What would others say if they were asked about whether you have a fixed or growth mindset? Would you dare to ask them?

Impact of fixed versus growth

As a result of your mindset, there are particular thoughts and behaviors that you are likely to experience. If you have a fixed mindset, you find it difficult to cope with challenges and especially with failures. You are overly concerned about how you will be judged, and you don't take risks. You value innate talent and capabilities but not effort. Overall, the fixed mindset is limiting and likely to create more stress, especially during challenging times.

If you have a growth mindset, you view challenges and failures as opportunities to learn. This doesn't necessarily make challenges and failures easy or desirable, but it does help you work your way through them and learn and develop as a result. Having a growth mindset, you value effort and take risks. The growth mindset is fulfilling and likely to create more calm and resolve during challenging times.

The good news about mindset

Dr. Dweck indicates that research shows that the most basic components of intelligence and personality traits can be changed, which supports the premise of the growth mindset. This is related to the concept of neuroplasticity, which I will discuss later in the book when it comes to stress management and which states that our brain is changeable. Therefore the good news: You can change your mindset.

How? Through awareness and through effort!

Everything in this book is about awareness and about effort, thus helping you develop your growth mindset further, or, if you happen to be caught in the fixed mindset, giving you the opportunity to switch to the growth mindset. You still need to jump at these opportunities, though! No one can make you jump!

The 360 degree feedback

You're probably aware of this tool, and you may have even gone through this process. If you haven't gone through it in recent years, going through it again might be an opportunity for growth.

The 360 Degree Feedback is a process in which employees receive confidential and anonymous feedback from the people around them. This typically includes the manager, peers, direct reports, and even people from the outside, such as customers, partners, and vendors. The questions typically cover a broad range of workplace competencies, with some responses utilizing a rating scale and some responses as free-form comments. The person receiving feedback also fills out the feedback form, which helps the person compare her perceptions of herself to how others perceive her.

The benefit of a 360 is that it can uncover personal strengths of which you may not be aware or that you are reluctant to claim, as well as weaknesses of which you may not be aware and potential fatal flaws that happen to be in your blind spot. As indicated earlier, you may also learn about your mindset and whether you have a fixed or growth mindset, which presents you with an opportunity to make some fundamental mindset changes.

A new phase in your leadership journey

The second phase of your leadership journey just started. "What was the first phase?" you might ask. And what is the second phase?

The first phase was focused on developing strengths, yours and others'. During this phase, we didn't mention or address weaknesses—except for the fatal flaw. The emphasis was on knowing your strengths, leveraging them, and building your confidence. It was also on noticing the strengths of others on your team and in your organization and helping them build their confidence, which you can only do if you are aware of and comfortable with your own strengths.

The second phase focuses on the growth mindset. The emphasis is on embracing your weaknesses and tackling them. Weaknesses are no longer weaknesses; they are opportunities for learning and growing. This phase is characterized by adopting the growth mindset, befriending challenges and weaknesses, and turning selected weaknesses into strengths.

You are invited to join us in the second phase and take your growth journey to the next level. There is a danger if you stay in phase one and stay focused on strengths. This actually may backfire, and like the fixed mindset, it limits your development and ability to adapt to a changing world. It is time you change the name of your Strengths Development Plan to Growth Plan and add one weakness that you would like to transform into a strength!

Behaviors, Behaviors, Behaviors

The results you have been getting at work, at home, in life, and in this leadership journey are largely determined by your mindset. If you have not been getting what you want, it is likely that the fixed mindset is playing a key role in that. If you reflect on this and discover that it is the fixed mindset that is standing in your way, first congratulate yourself for having discovered and acknowledged this, and then get into the "now what"! Here are three "now what" behaviors that you can start with:

Take a challenging problem and prepare the Problem Solving Matrix to help you practice problem solving and thinking of solutions, instead of becoming overwhelmed.

Take a difficult task and focus on it for thirty minutes. Start by preparing a Micro-Plan, and then work on one step at a time. Celebrate each step, and remember that the journey of one thousand miles starts with one step.

Take a difficult situation and go through the Awareness Wheel so you become aware of the underlying facts, thoughts, feelings, wants, and potential actions.

Each of these behaviors represents a small step from fixed to growth. If you accumulate enough of these steps, you will soon be making a leap into the growth mindset.

Chapter 8: Leading Collaboration, Innovation, and Change

In an increasingly complex and distributed work environment, the ability to lead collaboration, innovation, and change is vital, and no leadership effort is complete without it. Hence, it is time to discuss some important facets of collaboration, then dive into the topic of creativity and innovation, and conclude with the topic of leading change.

Collaboration tools

Are you and your team equipped with the tools and technologies that you need to collaborate, innovate, and manage change? If not, it would be fruitless to continue your work. Your effort is likely to be stymied and turned obsolete before it sees the light. If you still rely on e-mail and meetings to share information, discuss ideas, and manage projects, it is time you create a revolution in your team and your organization. It is time to introduce more effective and modern collaboration tools and technologies. This can be your next leadership project.

In our leadership program, for instance, we use a variety of collaboration tools to give leaders first-hand experience with these tools and equip them with valuable insights into how these tools can transform the workplace. We use an online portal with supporting material, assignments, online discussions, and progress tracking, all available 24x7. We use a wiki to publish meeting information and allow the participants to share their plans and co-create content. We have our live meetings via web conferencing and pre-scheduled office hours with faculty members. Participants use phone and in-person meetings as well as e-mail to coordinate and collaborate on their projects with learning partners. These are the tools that support collaboration, innovation, co-creation, information sharing, formal and informal learning, project management, and more.

Collaborative Problem Solving

With your collaboration tools and technologies in place, you are ready to tackle one of the core elements of successful collaboration: The ability to solve problems together. We talked about the Problem Solving Matrix in chapter 6 and used it as an individual tool to (a) break down problems into smaller components,

(b) strategize on how to address each component, (c) think through potential solutions, (d) identify the best option, and (e) come up with next steps. The same matrix can be turned into a collaborative problem-solving tool.

Get your team together in-person or virtually and identify a list of problems that need to be addressed. Rank these problems based on the chart that we introduced in chapter 6, and select a problem in the top right or top left quadrants. Introduce the Problem Solving Matrix and embark on facilitating an engaging problem-solving session while:

- Making sure that everyone is heard. It is easy for the expressive people to take over and miss the great ideas that others might have.

- Keeping the discussions focused on the Deltas. It is also easy for the Weak Links to take over. Your primary role as a leader is to keep bringing the discussion back to the Deltas.

- Applying a divide and conquer strategy to get the most accomplished. It is not necessary to discuss every aspect of the problem all together. Delegate certain items to the individuals or groups who are most familiar with or best positioned to tackle these items, and ask them to report back their findings.

While the above methodology provides a structure for problem solving and prepares your team for successful collaboration, the following discussion about creativity and innovation brings a whole new dimension to individual work and teamwork and will likely contribute tremendously to your leadership effort. After all, leadership is about creating and innovating; otherwise it may look more like managing than leading.

Creativity and Innovation—The Myth of the Lightning Bolt

In this section, Daniel Guillory, CEO of Innovations International, discusses this imperative topic of creativity and innovation, demystifying it and making it attainable to those who are willing to undertake such initiatives and create new and amazing outcomes. Daniel Guillory is a recognized expert on creativity and innovation, leadership and collaboration. Many different corporations and non-profits, including Toyota Financial Services, Ronald McDonald House Foundation, Merck & Co., and others, have turned to Daniel for his guidance on how to strategically approach these areas and for assistance in implementing tactical solutions in learning and development. Prior to working with Innovations, Daniel was an attorney with Pillsbury Madison & Sutro LLP and remains a member of the California Bar. He received his J.D. from Harvard Law School and his B.A. in International Relations from Stanford University.

Daniel notes that people seem to have the idea that creativity and innovation is often the insight that we seemingly receive from nowhere. We see the image of Archimedes in the bathtub and think that we can have that same experience.

And at times, Daniel states, we may experience that lightning bolt. But, more often than not, creativity is a deliberate, iterative process involving building the base of knowledge, challenging ideas, including the insight of others, and, for significant quantum jumps, actively exploring the unconscious. Here is Daniel's analysis on the creative process, followed by his insights on team creativity.

Pain and frustration

One myth we have is that the creative process is all fun. And certainly there are the moments when you are working in a stream of consciousness and thoughts are seemingly coming to you spontaneously. Or you are working in a team and suddenly feel alignment on a challenge that you have wrestled with for a long time.

However, the majority of the process is actually painful and frustrating. For example, it is painful when you share a new idea in a group and everyone tells you why it will not work. It is frustrating when you test your original idea or concept and it fails miserably. This is where more of the time is spent, much more so than in celebrating the new product or service that you believe will change the way business is done. So to be truly creative, be prepared to have a thick skin.

The reason for this goes to Picasso's famous quote, "Creativity is first of all an act of destruction." A creative act changes the way we do or view something—and by definition, most human beings do not embrace change. True creativity will often challenge something in which we have an interest, making us more resistant. It could be as simple as the resistance we get when we implement a new software solution that that will make the delivery of HR services more efficient, because people prefer the way they have always done it. Or it could be as large as when someone's role needs to change because the direction of the organization is different. People resist change, and creativity is the ultimate expression of change. Now that we have addressed the challenging part, let's talk about how to truly engage in the creative process.

Building the Base of knowledge—The Hard Skills

The ability to be truly creative in an area is directly proportional to the extent of your base of knowledge about that area. For example, the creative jump that my seven-year-old son can make in terms of his paintings would not compare to the kind of creative jump that someone like Claude Monet could make, who studied for years and years. If you study the work of many of the greatest artists, you will first find very simple drawings of the body, or one part of the body, done over and over again until a level of perfection was achieved. And these have typically been created long before the paintings or other works of art for which they are famous. The parallel is the same in sports—Lionel Messi is one of the most creative soccer players the world has seen, and when you watch him, you are often left asking yourself, "How did he do that?" But to be able to express himself creatively in that way, he first spent thousands of hours mastering very basic hard skills—the way you angle your foot when you pass a soccer ball, when you shoot a soccer ball, when you control a ball out of the air. Having the base of knowledge or hard skills is required before you can express true creativity about something.

Challenge and Feedback

Another essential part of the creative process is questioning and being able to receive feedback from others. Questioning is never easy to take. As someone who delivers workshops on creativity and innovation and encourages people to question others all of the time, when I am challenged by my team members, I find it sometimes difficult to receive. But many studies have shown that the creative results from this type of tension are actually stronger than in brainstorming environments where everyone's answer is considered equal and nothing is truly challenged.

This requires a certain level of personal development on our part—one of both confidence (I don't shrink immediately the first time I receive opinions different from what I believe) and of humility (even though I do believe in my idea, I am willing to see something from a different perspective). True creativity comes with being comfortable with tensions—comfort with being uncomfortable, openness to feedback yet confident in your idea, craving success yet willing to fail. It also requires a certain amount of trust and respect of those around you, because you are assuming that the people challenging your ideas have something of value to say.

Challenging is also enhanced by talking with people who may have a base of knowledge about my area but with a different focus. As someone in human resources, when I am working on a creative solution to something, do I ask people from the line businesses their opinion? Do I consult HR professionals from other industries? Do I get the perspective of someone from strategic planning or maybe someone from the study of psychology? These are all examples of individuals with a base of knowledge about people issues, but who see them from a very different perspective.

Using the Unconscious Mind

So once you have decided you are willing to endure the pain and frustrations, build your base of knowledge and hard skills, and engage in challenging questioning and feedback, what is next?

The unconscious mind offers us opportunities for truly unfettered exploration of new concepts and ideas. The more meditative our state—imagine a scale from fully awake, to day dreaming, to deep relaxation, to the sleep state—the less active our pre frontal cortex (rational decision-making part of our brain) is, and the more opportunity we give ourselves to explore. It is vital to remember that the range of our exploration depends directly on the work that we engaged in above. All of the research, studying, challenging, questioning, and receipt of feedback provide the foundation for us to explore.

And we have often done this exploration in the past. When I first experienced this in a memorable way was in high school. I spent all night working on a calculus problem that I could not answer and finally went to sleep at midnight, completely frustrated. When I awoke the next morning, I immediately knew the answer. I had not become more intelligent overnight, but my unconscious had gone thorough an exploration process that allowed me to return to my conscious state with an answer.

When most of us use the unconscious, we are not actively deciding its focus—itself selects based on its perspective of what is most important. As a result, here are some ways to "consciously direct your unconscious" (if that makes sense!):

1. Define the question: To begin to program our unconscious processes, we first need to give them a focus. Spend some time thinking about the question, opportunity, or challenge you are facing. Discuss it with a friend or colleague for feedback or clarification, and be open to the question changing over time as you engage in the creative process.

2. Seed your natural creative processes with the question: Once you have the question, ask yourself that question multiple times each day. There are natural creative triggers that we all have from which you will begin to get insights. Examples of these triggers that people have shared with me include when they are driving, running, swimming, showering, shaving, or washing their hair. We all have one or more of these triggers, so it is simply a matter of actively using them rather than them turning on or off independently.

3. Program the sleep state with your question: There are many books written on using sleep state creativity in which you can go into much greater detail on this topic. It is one of the most powerful processes available to you for extensive creative exploration. Essentially, you can ask yourself for an answer to your question each night before sleeping, and by interpreting your dreams the following day, gain greater and greater insight.

Each of these creative processes is of course iterative—the first answer you receive is unlikely to be the entire solution and may require multiple attempts. Often, the responses will come to you in series from which you will receive different parts at different times.

Creativity and Innovation are still fun and rewarding

We spent some time discussing the challenging aspects of creativity. That is simply because many people I encounter in my seminars want only the "fun" exercises but fail to recognize the time, effort, and energy required for true breakthrough creativity. At the same time, living on the edge of a current reality and creating a new one is, for me, one of the most enjoyable places to be in. It is fun, scary, daunting, challenging, frustrating, and rewarding at the same time. I invite you to engage in the journey.

Team Creativity

The first step in being creative is, of course, to proactively use and apply creativity on an individual basis. And as a necessity, one must be open to personal growth.

In addition to individual creativity, most of us work with others on creative processes in the workplace and do not simply create on our own. The requirements for group creativity are in some ways more challenging than for individual creativity, as I will discuss below.

Actively seek people outside of my comfort zone

This first step is a challenge because one is actually required to seek difference, as in difference in ideas and opinions. This is at first a difficult task because it is rarely in our nature to seek out people with whom we may have conflict and disagreement. And yet it is such an essential element of the creative process. The various types of dimensions of difference that we could consider include thinking style, work style, educational background, nationality, race, ethnicity, sex, and communication style. This is a small sample of the list of differences that we could select, but it gives you a sense of some of the business critical dimensions of diversity that are available to us as creative inputs, if we choose to take advantage of them. The dimensions we select may have some relation to the objective of our project, but we may want to even consider some that we do not believe to be directly related to the goal, as they may offer surprises that cannot be predicted in advance.

Of the different dimensions, the two that most commonly relate to those that we include or exclude in the workplace are work style and thinking style. It is a subtle distinction for us to evaluate people on the result itself rather than focusing on how they achieve the result. Consider how often each of us has started to discount what someone was in the process of achieving, well before they were even complete, because of how they were approaching a task that:

- Was too linear

- Involved too much discussion

- Took too long because someone wanted to reach consensus

- Went too fast because no one was consulted

- Focused too much on details

- Spent too much time on the big picture and not enough on details

- Was not sensitive to people's feelings

- Tried unproductively to satisfy everyone

These are each examples of characteristics that can be strengths in different circumstances and can contribute to the creative process—but also where we require a truly heightened level of awareness to ensure that we are actively seeking out these differences when working together.

Be open to personal growth and know that my reality will change

We need to understand that we are going to experience transformation, whether it is when we engage in individual creativity or group creativity. The gulf of transformation from one reality to another, however, will likely be more dramatic when we work with others, since they bring a whole different set of experiences and perspectives. Although it is true that what people create together may be more powerful, that very creation will inevitably invalidate long held beliefs, values, and truths that each individual may have, making an impact in many areas of life.

Embrace conflict

This seems like a tall order, since conflict is rarely fun. However to help with the process, there are a few key ideas one can use. A great practice is that when trying to critique a person's idea, one should try to suggest something that would make the original idea more effective in that person's opinion. In that way two things are achieved. First, the process is additive, and ideas are being advanced rather than simply deconstructed. Second, it requires more advanced thinking and true evaluation of a concept. It is very easy to identify what one believes are the weaknesses in something, but to authentically (and in an in-depth way) evaluate in an attempt to modify is a much more involved process. Conflict and disagreement will naturally be a part of any creative process, and the key is to manage it in a way that continues to move forward toward a creative solution.

Ensure contributions from all team members

Team members have very different styles, and as a result, it takes an active conscious effort to ensure contributions from everyone. Some people may actively participate immediately, while others may prefer to reflect and find moments where they can share their thoughts in a one-on-one way with different individuals. As a result, when designing a creative team process, it is important to design opportunities to ensure everyone can participate. Combine traditional group discussions with opportunities that require everyone to individually present their perspective on a challenge in an in-depth way, or even opportunities for people to share their perspective in pairs or in small groups before reporting to a larger group. It can also be helpful to provide different media for people to display their perspectives visually through tools such as mind mapping, as many people tend to process things in different ways (some visually through imagery, others through spoken word, and others through written word).

Use limitations strategically

Limitations such as space, resources, and time can often serve as a spark for creativity and innovation. When groups are forced into challenging situations, they often are able to develop very new, innovative solutions to problems that they would not have otherwise considered. Although some people have the self-mastery to push themselves, many find their greatest levels of creativity when pushed by outside demands.

Team creativity is one of the most powerful processes available if people are leveraged correctly and prepared to experience personal growth in the process.

Leading Change

Daniel's discussion above about creativity and innovation provided valuable insights and helped demystify this process, equipping you with concepts and techniques that can help augment creativity and innovation and lead your team to embrace it. However, with creativity and innovation comes change. Therefore, leading change and helping people overcome internal and external obstacles is yet another necessary leadership skill and set of behaviors. Change is not only associated with creativity and innovation, though. It is an inherent part of our lives, be it business or personal. This makes the topic of leading change even more pertinent.

So much has been written already about change and change management. It is not my intention to reiterate the change management literature or reinvent change management. Instead, I intend to present a few innovative models that are largely based on research and breakthrough scientific findings and translate them into helpful concepts and behaviors that can add to your behavioral repertoire. These concepts and behaviors will help you tackle change at the individual, team, and organizational level.

The SCARF model by David Rock

In 2008, David Rock, CEO of Results Coaching Systems International and Co-Founder of NeuroLeadership Institute, introduced SCARF[15], a brain-based model for collaborating with and influencing others. The foundation of this model, which is built on research by Evian Gordon, is that our social behavior is governed by an underlying principle of the brain to minimize threat and maximize reward.[16]

When the brain receives a stimulus, it will tag it as "bad" or "good" (threat or reward) and then react accordingly, with an attempt to avoid "bad" things and approach "good" things. Research has shown that our reactions to a stimulus are governed by the same brain networks and result in the same physiological and emotional symptoms whether the stimulus is a result of a lion chasing us in the forest or our boss making a negative comment about our performance. This means that a threat, perceived or real, causes a similar set of reactions. These reactions are meant to protect us, which is quite necessary in the case of a lion but not applicable nor necessary in the case of the boss's comment.

The amygdala, which is part of the limbic system in the brain, plays a key role in identifying threats and rewards and in responding to them. When a threat is detected by the limbic system (the amygdala), this system engages our basic survival mechanisms and disengages our conscious thought process in the prefrontal cortex. This translates into a diminished ability to think straight, communicate intelligently, solve complex problems, and make good

---

[15] For details about SCARF, refer to the report "SCARF: a brain-based model for collaborating with and influencing others" by David Rock, first published in the *NeuroLeadership Journal* (2008)

[16] Evian Gordon, *Integrative Neuroscience: Bringing together biological, psychological and clinical models of the human brain* (Singapore: Harwood Academic Publishers, 2000)

decisions, among other things. Ironically, these are exactly the functions we need in such a threatening situation.

On the other hand, when we perceive a reward, we get motivated and engaged. Different mechanisms get triggered in our brain. This translates into increased levels of dopamine, which is a neurotransmitter important for interest and learning and several other functions. This means increased ability for problem solving, decision making, communication, and the like.

David Rock's SCARF module highlights five areas in which we are likely to perceive threats or rewards: status, certainty, autonomy, relatedness, and fairness (hence the designation SCARF). David Rock explains, "Status is about relative importance to others. Certainty concerns being able to predict the future. Autonomy provides a sense of control over events. Relatedness is a sense of safety with others, of friend rather than foe. And fairness is a perception of fair exchanges between people."

When collaborating with others and when leading change, being attentive to the five areas of the SCARF model and understanding how you and your team perceive threats and rewards in each of these areas can help you plan ways to minimize threats and create rewards, therefore improving collaboration and effectively leading change. Let us consider each of the areas of the SCARF model and shed some light on their applications.

Status

Status is about relative importance and seniority, indicates David Rock. Our perception of status when interacting with others can lead to perceived threats or rewards and impact our mental processes and behaviors. Even the slightest indication that our status is threatened, possibly by something as simple as a remark someone has made, can trigger a chain of undesirable reactions. Therefore, being attentive to status is critical in each and every interaction. Performance reviews and giving feedback are especially delicate in that they tend to elicit the status threat response easily, even when they are not meant to do so. Finding ways to engage the person is key. Asking questions and seeking their point of view can help.

Promotions, nice offices, and pay increases are obvious ways to reward people and establish status. However, they may or may not be within reach, and they may even lead to complications if, for instance, the person being promoted is not necessarily able to perform well in the new role. The good news is that there are other ways to reward status, such as giving public acknowledgement. This is even more important during periods of change when other factors may be difficult to control, yet acknowledging individuals for their contributions is possible and effective.

Certainty

The brain is a pattern-recognizing machine, indicates David Rock, and likes to know the patterns occurring moment to moment so that it can predict what is next. Without patterns and without prediction, which is what uncertainty brings about, every situation would be a new situation, and it would require energy, especially thinking-energy on the part of the prefrontal cortex. Uncertainty therefore is perceived as a threat. Even small levels of uncertainty can create that perception, while a higher level of uncertainty, such as with job performance or job security, can be perceived as a significant threat.

While there are uncertainties that are difficult to control, focusing on the uncertainties where we can achieve some level of planning and of setting expectations can go a long way in enhancing our overall sense of certainty. Many of the leadership tools that we discussed throughout this book are designed to help achieve some level of certainty during uncertain times and situations. The Immediate Priorities Matrix lays out more clearly what our world looks like now and allows us to plan and address related uncertainties by setting expectations and negotiation. The End Results Matrix helps create a vision for the next few months, also creating some level of certainty. At the micro level, Micro-Planning helps solidify the path that will lead to a successful completion of the task at hand. In addition to that are the Problem Solving Matrix and the Negotiation Matrix, both designed to prepare you to manoeuver through difficult and uncertain situations. One more tool that is highly effective during uncertain times is the Awareness Wheel, helping you engage the prefrontal cortex and uncover the interpretations and assumptions that are leading to the perception of threats.

Autonomy

Autonomy is about the perception of having control and having choices. This explains why micro-management is counter-productive. This also explains why collaboration and teamwork can be challenging, especially for those who are high on autonomy, meaning those who value autonomy more so than the other five areas in the SCARF model. It is important to note, however, that collaboration and teamwork increase one's perception of status and relatedness, which might compensate for the decrease in autonomy.

Giving people choices and options instead of instructions and directions is one way to help create some degree of autonomy. Similar to certainty, even though it is not typically possible or practical to create a high level of autonomy, it is still quite satisfying and fulfilling to allow autonomy in certain areas or aspects of a person's work. For instance, while the project deliverables may be dictated by the client, the approach or the way of structuring the work can still be delegated to the people responsible for doing the work. Finding creative ways to provide even small doses of autonomy is an essential part of motivating people and helping them innovate, collaborate, and manage change.

Relatedness

Relatedness concerns the concept of being inside or outside a social group, which translates into whether one is welcome and perceived as belonging or not welcome and perceived as a stranger or even a threat. The perception of someone as "in" or "out" translates into the reward or threat responses discussed earlier. Relatedness is linked to trust, indicates David Rock. Therefore trust-building activities create relatedness and, of course, behaviors that are untrustworthy take away from relatedness.

Team-building activities, social activities, and water cooler conversations all increase relatedness and help build trust, which, in turn, leads to increased collaboration, enhanced productivity, and better handling of challenges during change. Mentoring, peer coaching, and all aspects of informal learning help reinforce and deepen relatedness. Research also points out that relatedness is not about quantity. David Rock observes that perhaps even one trusting relationship suffices to create relatedness.

Fairness

Unfair exchanges can generate significant threat responses, while fair exchanges can result in perceived rewards. Increasing transparency, establishing clear roles and responsibilities, having best practices and guidelines, and setting expectations clearly can help establish a higher sense of fairness. Enabling team members to participate in creating best practices and guidelines can contribute not only to fairness but also to autonomy and certainty.

The *Switch* model

Switch: How to Change Things When Change Is Hard is a bestselling book by Chip and Dan Heath about making lasting change in all facets of life.[17] The *Switch* framework recognizes two important aspects of our psyche that largely influence our behaviors. One is the rational side, which tends to analyze situations and formulate future plans, while the other is the emotional side responsible for the myriad of feelings that we experience. Our rational and emotional sides are, as described in *Switch*, similar to an elephant and a rider in that they need to work together in order to achieve successful outcomes. However, they have different interests and styles and therefore may not agree on what to do or how to do it.

The Rider (our rational side) has significant strength, such as the ability to think long term and to plan. However, it also has significant weaknesses, such as getting into the analysis paralysis mode and overthinking situations, instead of forging ahead. The Elephant (our emotional side), on the other hand, displays love, compassion, sympathy, loyalty, and energy—all important aspects of getting motivated and taking action and especially useful during periods of change. However, it also has some serious weaknesses in that it is hungry for instant gratification and therefore can get lazy and distracted.

---

[17] Chip Heath and Dan Heath, *Switch: How to Change Things When Change Is Hard* (New York: Broadway Books, 2010)

Knowing that change requires short-term sacrifices for long-term gains, when change fails, it is usually because of the Elephant's hunger for instant gratification. *Switch* explains that if you have slept in, overeaten, procrastinated, tried to quit smoking and failed, skipped the gym, gotten angry and said something you regretted, abandoned your Spanish or piano lessons, or refused to speak up in a meeting, it is likely that the Elephant is behind these behaviors. The Rider, however, can also slow down change if it can't decide and gets into the analysis paralysis mode.

For change to happen successfully, you need to appeal to both—the Rider and the Elephant.

Jon Stegner: Appealing to the Elephant, Not just the Rider

One of the case studies highlighted in *Switch* is the story of Jon Stegner, who believed that his company was incurring substantial and unnecessary costs procuring different types of work gloves from different vendors instead of standardizing on vendors, types of gloves, and one procurement process. To reduce this huge operational expense would require a big process shift and would require convincing the management team and the presidents of the business units in question.

With the help of an intern, Stegner identified all the types of gloves used at the company and the cost associated with each, which amounted to more than four hundred types from different vendors and at varying costs. He collected specimens of these gloves in one boardroom and displayed them with price tags. Then he invited all the presidents to come and see first-hand this undisputable display of a process that went out of control. The reaction was one of disbelief. Soon he got the firm mandate that he was seeking: This process needs to be changed.

Most people in Stegner's situation would have made a presentation with spreadsheets and charts that would appeal mostly to the Rider. But Stegner knew that he needed to get the Elephant on his side, as well to create an immediate and lasting impact. The boardroom full of gloves accomplished exactly that.

The Switch framework: Rider, Elephant, Path

The *Switch* framework includes three elements:

First: Directing the Rider. What looks like resistance to change is often lack of clarity. Providing the Rider with clarity and helping the Rider overcome the analysis paralysis paves the road for a successful change effort when this effort is combined with the following two elements.

Second: Motivating the Elephant. Engaging people's emotional side by allowing them to relate the change to issues and values they are passionate about and they can feel for.

Third: Shaping the Path. What looks like a people problem is often a situation problem. By improving the situation and/or formulating the step-by-step process when applicable, change becomes digestible and feasible.

Donald Berwick in Healthcare

Donald Berwick is referred to in *Switch* as the man who changed the face of healthcare. Berwick headed the Institute of Health Care Improvements and was determined to address the high "defect" rate, meaning medical mistakes that often led to fatalities, in healthcare, estimated at the time to be one in ten. In December 2004, Berwick boldly announced an ambitious vision for healthcare professionals: "We should save 100,000 lives by June 14, 2006." During his speech, he was joined by the mother of a girl who was killed in error during a hospitalization. You can see that Berwick understood the importance of motivating the Elephant (the second element of the *Switch* framework). He didn't just talk numbers; he wanted to engage people's emotions and passion toward an extremely important topic literally affecting patients' lives.

Hearing Berwick's announcement, the crowd was astounded and overwhelmed by the goal. Berwick and his team proposed six interventions to save lives. Over 1000 hospitals were soon enrolled. This was an enormous undertaking. Hospitals needed to change processes and behaviors. Berwick and his team made it happen. June 14, 2006, at 9:00 am, Berwick took the stage again and announced success: "An estimated 122,300 lives were saved." Berwick created this remarkable change even though he had no authority over these hospitals. Here is what he did:

First: He directed his audience's Rider. The destination was crystal clear. He didn't simply indicate that they need to save many lives soon. He stated 100,000 lives by June 14, 2006. But that wasn't all. He and his team proposed six specific interventions that hospitals could implement to help achieve this vision.

Second: He motivated his audience's Elephant. Many of them already knew the facts, but knowing was not enough. He brought his audience face-to-face with the mother of the girl who was killed by a medical error ("I know that if this campaign had been in place four or five years ago, that Josie would be fine," she said).

Third: He shaped the Path. He made it easy for hospitals to join. He provided step-by-step instructions, assigned mentors, and connected people together to help create a community and a shared mission.

The Accomplishing More Leadership Program model

The Accomplishing More Leadership Program, to which this book is a companion, lays out the model, summarized below, for leading change:

First, recognize and acknowledge people's strengths, including your own. Amazing transformations happen when we focus on strengths instead of weaknesses. If you want people to change, start by recognizing and acknowledging their strengths. This is the prerequisite for change. This helps to minimize the threats that are typically associated with change and to accumulate rewards that can be later drawn upon during periods of change. This addresses the five areas highlighted earlier in the SCARF model: status, certainty, autonomy, relatedness, and fairness. Strengths build status, help create certainty, can lead to increased autonomy, enable people to feel connected and therefore increase relatedness, and, finally, contribute to people being treated equitably, therefore increasing fairness.

Second, grow and develop the growth mindset. This is only possible after having recognized and acknowledged strengths. This is also a required next step. If we stop at recognizing and acknowledging strengths, we risk cultivating satisfaction with the status quo or even arrogance, both detrimental to change and leading change. The growth mindset discussed previously is an important pillar for persevering through the challenges associated with innovation and change.

Third, transform the fundamental limiting thoughts that may be contributing to resistance to change, to significant stress, and to less than desirable results, which is the topic of the next chapter.

Behaviors, Behaviors, Behaviors

This chapter presented a broad range of concepts, models, and behaviors related to collaboration, innovation, and change. It is time to put these to work. The collaborative problem-solving approach described above is a great place to start. Every collaboration effort is likely to face challenges of one kind or another. Consider one of the challenges that your team is facing, and initiate and lead a collaborative problem-solving session.

Review the innovation and creativity principles presented above, and reflect on the state of innovation and creativity in your current environment. Identify steps that you can take to enhance such effort. Innovation and creativity are appealing topics for most people. You are likely to get some traction and create some momentum in your team as you undertake such initiatives.

When it comes to leading change, start small and gradually work your way to tackling the bigger change initiatives. First identify some practices and behaviors that can help you better understand the models discussed. As you gain experience with these practices and behaviors, you will be ready to undertake the more significant effort.

Chapter 9: Wrestling Stress Like a Ninja

More than 95 percent of our leadership survey participants indicated that effective stress management is an important leadership trait. We agree. Leaders diffuse stress instead of propagating it. They turn stress into understanding and into action. In the presence of leaders, people feel less stress, and as a result of the leaders' behaviors and coaching, people become more effective at managing stress.

We already tackled a multitude of stress management techniques for leaders ranging from (a) ways to manage the information overload and the resulting stress, such as using the Immediate Priorities Matrix to sort competing and overwhelming priorities, treating e-mail as a task and feeling in control instead of out of control, and working in bursts instead of feeling pulled in different direction at all times to (b) working more effectively with people through understanding personality and leadership styles and conducting effective negotiation and collaborative problem solving to (c) deploying the awareness wheel to make difficult and stressful situations manageable and actionable, especially when they related to inter-personal conflict and communication issues.

In this chapter, Dr. Alicia Ruelaz Maher takes stress management to a whole new level, introducing the mental and physical aspects of stress, the neurological phenomena behind stress, and what we can do to overcome the root causes of stress. Dr. Maher is a Board Certified Diplomate of the American Board of Psychiatry and Neurology, with subspecialty certification in Psychosomatic Medicine. Dr. Maher translates her knowledge of neuroscience into tools and techniques that can enhance individual lives. In addition to over fifteen years of working with patients, she also taught medical students as Assistant Clinical Professor at the University of California, San Francisco and the University of California, Los Angeles, and she defines the state of practice through cutting-edge research with the RAND Corporation. Dr. Maher has lectured to thousands of professionals on a variety of topics. She is particularly passionate about helping people to rewire their brains in order to experience their maximum potential.

What is stress?

We've all heard the word stress thrown around enough that probably no one is wondering what it is. But looking at some definitions can still help us truly understand this important phenomenon. The original definition, according to physics, is the "application of a sufficient force to an object to distort it." That makes sense and is the simplified picture of stress that people want to believe. Here you are, this object, and all of these forces or circumstances are acting on you to ruin what would otherwise be peaceful days and happy productivity.

What we know now is that stress is not that simple. It's not so much what is going on around you but, rather, what is going on in the brain. The definition from physics makes perfect sense when you are thinking of applying a force to a metal pipe. However, humans, as you can imagine, have the luxury of being more complicated. When it comes to us humans, what is occurring in the mind is actually far more important than what is actually occurring. So, for us, stress is a condition or feeling experienced when a person perceives that demands upon them exceed the personal and social resources the individual is able to mobilize. They key word here is "perceives."

What we found is that regardless of the experiences in our lives, the way we approach or evaluate them mentally is what actually has the biggest effect on us. What this means is that often two people can go through the same experience and one will suffer the effects of stress while the other will not. You can probably imagine several activities, like roller coasters, skydiving, violent movies, etc., that some people find exciting, while others want to avoid them at all costs. Another example, for instance, relates to financial stability. Two people may have the same level of financial resources, but for one, finances cause a lot of stress, while for the other, finances are not even an issue. In essence, our perception is what defines our experience and our stress.

Mental Stress

Mental stress impacts us physically. What happens in the brain causes reactions within the physical body through alterations in neurochemicals and hormones. Think about how quickly your heart might start pounding and your palms might start sweating if you're called on in a meeting and feel put on the spot or if you're about to give a speech to a large and unfamiliar audience—or whatever the situation is for you.

What happens as a result of your thoughts about the event is that neurochemicals and hormones are released, and they affect a number of bodily functions, including your glucose metabolism releasing nutrients stored in muscles to provide energy, your cardiac output increasing blood flow to muscles, and your blood pressure rising, to name just a few. By the way, this response is important when a lion is chasing you but probably doesn't help much with the stressors of today. In addition, when a lion is chasing you, this response goes away once the lion goes away. Thoughts however, unlike a real event that ends, keep happening, and therefore we experience a constant activation of this system, which is wearing our bodies down and causing significant damage.

If we don't identify those thoughts and stop or change them to something more positive, we are likely to suffer as a result. If, however, we change these thoughts and stop the neurochemicals and stress hormones from being released, imagine the greater health, energy, and productivity we could experience. This is our goal!

In addition to the thoughts that we are aware of, there are numerous thoughts that we are not aware of. If we're not actively thinking, our brain is always passively receiving information and cycling through it subconsciously, which is having an effect on us. Consider advertising, for instance. We're constantly receiving messages and internalizing them. We see hundreds of ads each week, and we are bombarded by messages about how life should be and the perfect this and that. Subconsciously, we make comparisons, which lead to having thoughts that we're not okay or that our lives are not ideal, causing an unrecognized background level of distress.

Our thoughts determine our life

So thoughts determine how we feel, particularly whether we will release the neurochemicals and hormones associated with stress. Besides how we feel, our thoughts and beliefs can lead to different actions. If you don't think a movie will be good, you won't watch it. If you don't think there is any way you can get a particular job, you probably won't apply for it. So our beliefs are also determining our actions and our reality. Therefore, we want to be careful that our beliefs aren't determining a reality that we don't like.

If we don't have the energy, peacefulness, and productivity that we desire, there is probably something going on in our thoughts that needs to be recognized. The same goes for feeling stressed. If we are feeling overly stressed, there is probably something going on in our thoughts that needs to be recognized.

If we don't uncover the negative thoughts and replace them with more positive ones, we are likely to be tormented under the weight of our thoughts. Another way of saying this is that if we don't control our thoughts, they will control us.

Cognitive Behavioral Theory

This theory states that by examining our thoughts, we can know why our emotions are going in a certain direction and why we feel stressed, and then we can guide our thoughts in the direction we desire. According to this theory, it's not important to understand why you have the experience of anxiety in certain situations, like if something happened in your childhood or whatever else might be the case; it is more important to uncover the underlying thoughts, which are typically distorted and exaggerated, and then replace them with more realistic thoughts. Here are some of the common cognitive distortions behind our negative thoughts that cause our stress:

1. All-or-nothing thinking: You only see things in black and white. For instance, if your performance falls short of perfect, you see yourself as a total failure.

2. Overgeneralization: You see a single negative event as a never-ending pattern of defeat. If a bird craps on your

window, you think that they are always crapping on your window, ignoring the many days that they haven't.

3. Mental filtering: You pick out a single negative detail and dwell on it exclusively, so that your vision of all reality becomes darkened. This is similar to the drop of ink that discolors the entire glass of water. For instance, even if someone says five nice things to you, you only focus on the one bit of constructive criticism that was said and ignore all the positive.

4. Disqualifying the positive: In this case, you reject positive experiences, by insisting they "don't count" for some reason or other. For instance, someone giving you a compliment is "just being nice." You maintain a negative belief, even if it is contradicted by your everyday experiences.

5. Jumping to conclusions: You make a negative interpretation, even though there are no definite facts that convincingly support your conclusion. Two popular forms of jumping to conclusions are mind reading, where you assume what someone is thinking or what the motivation is behind their actions, and fortune telling, where you assume a negative outcome for an event as if you know it for sure.

6. Catastrophizing (also called magnification and minimization): You exaggerate the importance of things, such as your goof-up or someone else's achievement. Or you inappropriately shrink things, such as your own desirable qualities or others' imperfections, which is also referred to as the binocular trick.

7. Emotional reasoning: You assume that your negative emotions reflect the way things really are: "I feel it, therefore it must be true."

8. Should statements: With should statements, you try to motivate yourself by having many shoulds and shouldn'ts, as if you had to be whipped and punished before you could be expected to do anything. Another variation is to have many shoulds and shouldn'ts about the world and people, as if the world and people are meant to satisfy your own needs.

9. Labeling: instead of describing an error, you attach a label, such as "I'm a loser" or "He's a jerk."

10. Personalization: You assume yourself to be responsible for an outside event. You confuse influence with control. For instance, my child got an F because I am a terrible mother.

Cognitive Distortions in Action

The area where these distortions come out most dramatically is in evaluating patients for suicide. I (Dr. Maher) remember one day when I had to see an older lady who was in the ICU after overdosing on pills. Her eyesight was failing, so that she could no longer read books. She decided she couldn't possibly be happy without being able to read, and so she attempted suicide. Which distortion would that be? This is mental filtering.

Dr. Jonathan Drummond was a paediatric heart surgeon who implanted life-saving miniature heart pumps in children. On Christmas Day, 2004, at the age of forty-five, he overdosed on alcohol and pain medication. The CEO of his hospital stated that some doctors would say they saved ninety-eight out of a hundred lives, but Dr. Drummond looked at it and said that he lost two. Which cognitive distortions apply here? This is all-or-nothing thinking and mental filtering.

Here are some common situations for you to reflect on and identify which cognitive distortion is involved in each:

- I can't believe that idiot just cut me off!

- I will never make it to work with all of this traffic.

- I shouldn't be upset.

These involve labeling, jumping to conclusions, and should statements, respectively.

Overcoming Mental Stress

Noticing that you have thoughts that may be causing problems for you is a good start. Now you have something to work on. The world of neuroscience has shown that we can actually do something to alter these thoughts. We can alter how our brains work. This is known as neuroplasticity or how changeable the brain is. Much like how we can work on our bodies by choosing to exercise certain parts and get them to be stronger, we can change how our brain works and make it stronger.

Our brain cells

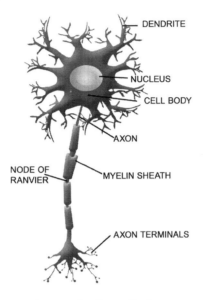

Our brains are made up of cells, called neurons, like the ones pictured above. When we have thoughts and experiences, those neurons pass a neurochemical message to other neurons, which leads to emotions and behaviors. As a result, the branches around the neuron bodies, called dendrites, grow. They grow as they get used.

If you learn something new and you experience an aha moment, you are actually sensing the new connection being formed between the neurons. If you continue to think thoughts and practice behaviors along the same lines as the new connection, you strengthen it. If you don't, the dendrites retract and the connection or brilliant insight goes away in favor of older or stronger patterns.

Therefore, according to neuroplasticity, (a) we can adopt new thoughts and behaviors, creating new connections in our brain, and thus alter our brain, and (b) we can maintain these new alterations by practicing the new thoughts and behaviors and stopping the reinforcement of the old ones.

Transforming thoughts

So how do we transform the problematic thoughts that we identify? Well, we can't just slap a happy face sticker on them and make them go away. We can't actually replace a negative thought with a positive one so easily. If your thought is "I'm a loser," saying "I'm a winner" is not going to have much effect. In order to make those neurons fire and form a new connection, there must be some feeling behind the new thought. Thoughts without feelings don't produce much of a neurochemical reaction. In addition, it is difficult to transform a negative thought to a positive thought all at once. It is more realistic to attempt a small incremental transformation at first.

Therefore you don't have to go from "No one likes me" to "Everyone likes me" in order to feel better. You just have to find something slightly more positive that you also believe in, such as "My neighbor likes me." If you believe that your neighbor likes you, you can't simultaneously strongly believe that no one likes you. You've just given yourself evidence that the belief that no one likes you isn't true. If you feel a little relief with the new statement, this indicates that there is a feeling behind it and that a new connection between the neurons took place. Once this new thought becomes habit, you can go on to create the next incremental transformation.

As you tackle the thought transformation process, I recommend you start by ranking your negative thoughts on scale of one to ten, one being an extremely negative thought that is causing extreme stress and ten being a very positive thought that is leading to enthusiasm and happiness. The thought of "No one likes me," for instance, may be ranked as three on this scale. It's definitely not calm, but it is not nervous breakdown either. Then try to come up with a more positive thought that can help you move from a three to a four. Remember that it needs to be a thought that you believe for the neuronal connection to form. The "My neighbor likes me" thought fits just right in this case, assuming that you feel some relief as a result.

As you notice the thoughts passing through your head throughout the day, ask yourself, "Do I want this thought to be creating my life?" See if that thought is leading you closer to your desired outcome or your undesired outcome, and if necessary, gently guide your thoughts toward something more pleasant.

As you go through this process, keep in mind that your negative thought is likely to have one or more cognitive distortions. By examining these distortions and disputing them, you are likely to find the more realistic and more positive replacement thought.

Transforming subconscious thoughts

The process of transforming negative thoughts requires that you first identify these thoughts. How about situations in which you experience stress or some feeling of background anxiety but can't find the underlying thoughts that are causing the stress or the anxiety? How do you get to peacefulness in this case? Let us look into a practice known by many as mindfulness. Mindfulness involves recognizing what is going on around you, without reacting to it. Mindfulness practices can move our brains toward being less stressed and more productive.

I want you to close your eyes and make yourself as comfortable as you can. Take a deep breath in, and let it out slowly. Paying attention to your breath, I want you to breathe deeply and slowly, allowing yourself to become more and more relaxed. As you slip into this relaxed state, notice the chair you are sitting on. Feel the weight of your body supported by this chair. Notice any air movement or breeze that touches your skin.

If any thoughts start to arise, I want you to just label them thoughts and let them drift on by like clouds in the sky. Return to focusing on your breathing. Now, notice if any sounds arise. Rather than thinking about the sound, just label that sound a sound and let it be. Notice the sounds, notice any thoughts, notice your body and allow everything to be the way it is, without judging it or trying to change it. For just these couple of minutes, allow yourself to relax completely and just be.

In a way, mindfulness is the ability to be in the present moment without distraction. Mindfulness techniques cause one to pay attention to his or her present thoughts, body sensations, emotions, without passing judgment or reacting. Mindfulness is important because typically, so much of what is going on in our heads is compulsive thinking about the future or the past. We miss out on actual life because we're too busy planning for the next thing. We can make a difficult time much worse for ourselves, if we continue to overthink it.

Often, there's no problem in the present. I have been extremely upset at times, but when I look around me and engage my senses, I realize that, right now, in this moment, there is no problem. The ultimate goal is to incorporate mindfulness into all areas of your life, to notice when you are out of the present moment, and to engage your senses to get back into it.

Physical Stress

The brain perceives something as stressful (like a snake about to bite me), and this causes the body to be activated. This is what we call fight or flight—basically our body is activated to prepare us to respond by fighting the danger or running away from it. The activation of our body includes all kinds of bodily functions and symptoms, including an increase in heart rate, blood pressure, and oxygen and glucose delivery to tissues, as well as possibly sweating, excitability, and more.

As I mentioned earlier, if you were called on in a meeting or about to give a speech to a large and unfamiliar audience, you might experience such symptoms. These symptoms are involuntary, produced automatically by the part of our nervous system that isn't under our voluntary control. This is the nervous system that takes care of digestion, blood vessels opening and closing, etc.—things we don't have to think about.

This is what makes stress difficult to manage. If we perceive something as stressful, we automatically go into this response, seemingly without any control. What makes it even more difficult is that it isn't just fight or flight. This reaction has been more recently renamed as fight, flight, or freeze. Freezing is helpful if you're walking through a forest and hear a lion. You brace yourself and hold your breath, in the hope that you won't call attention to yourself and that the lion will walk on by. However, with today's stressors, freeze is counterproductive. While we mostly don't notice it, we tend to tense our muscles and hold our breath all throughout the day, in reaction to stressful thoughts of which we probably aren't even conscious. This leads to much of the tension and fatigue that we experience. What can we do to remedy this physical stress? Here is where the voluntary nervous system comes to the rescue.

Besides the involuntary nervous system, we obviously have another part of the nervous system that is under our voluntary control. This is how we're able to move our arms and legs and do the things we want to do. We can use our voluntary nervous system to counteract what our body might be doing involuntarily.

This is similar to transforming thoughts, in a way. I previously discussed recognizing negative thoughts and transforming them. In this case, it is about learning to recognize the physical symptoms of stress, which are caused by the involuntary nervous system, and then to counteract them using the voluntary nervous system.

How stress affects the body

Why should we care about doing something to counteract these symptoms, which are caused by a natural process? Because in addition to stress not feeling good, there is actually quite a bit of physical danger in stress. And it is important to understand the ways in which specific stressors translate to specific physical dangers. The more we understand about the specifics of stress and illness, the more accurately we can counteract that stress. There are many areas that we could look at, but we are just going to focus on a few, starting with cardiovascular disease.

Cardiovascular disease

While all of the diseases I'm discussing are important, cardiovascular disease is the leading cause of death in the U.S. among men and women. Looking at cardiovascular disease, this involves plaque that build up in the vessels, especially the small coronary arteries that supply the heart. Just like clogging a hose reduces the amount of water that comes out, plaque buildup causes less blood to flow, and therefore less oxygen will be able to get to the heart muscle.

Stress activates the fight or flight nervous system, and that activation increases inflammation and plaque development. So in addition to causing the heart to beat faster and increasing the work that the heart needs to do, stress also promotes the plaque development and therefore makes the heart unable to meet the increased demand. You see how this is a problem, right? Plaque buildup, coupled with the increased demand on the heart, can cause a heart attack.

There are certain stressors that seem most predictive of heart disease. They seem to particularly relate to work stress, and not just any work stress. Research found that the risk of cardiovascular disease is 50 percent higher if we experience high demands with little control, or inadequate compensation, and/or organizational injustice. However, it is not that these stressors happen and cause cardiovascular disease. They cause the disease to people with a certain way of relating to the world, a certain psychological makeup. We previously called these people Type A, and now we refer to them as having a personality based on anger, hostility, and aggressiveness.

This psychological makeup can be as strongly detrimental as the effects of smoking and poor diets, according to some studies. It is believed that reacting to the world in this way is mediated by exaggerated neurochemical and neurohormonal responses.

There are things that can be done to alter this type of psychological makeup. If the condition is extreme, this should probably be done through counseling that would involve examining habitual thoughts and beliefs that promote hostility and impatience, helping the person, for instance, to detect early warning signals that they're about to get angry and to better understand and cope with these reactions. Remembering that these thoughts and behaviors are going to lead to disease usually motivates the person to change them.

Other approaches include rearranging one's life in order to get out of situations that are overwhelming or training oneself to take more constructive actions using some of the methods I talked about earlier, such as transforming thoughts or meditation practices. You may also be happy to know that aspirin also seems to protect the heart via decreased blood clots and may also decrease inflammation.

Immunity

Stress' effects on immunity are related to the fact that the stress hormone cortisol decreases immunity when it is released in bursts. Normally, this should be short-lived, and it should go back to normal when we're done dealing with the actual stressors. However, many of the stressors that we face today are caused by our own thoughts, which tend to keep happening, and therefore lead to long periods of cortisol release and further damage to the immune system.

Passive stress seems to cause the greatest amount of cortisol release and therefore the greatest effect on immunity. Passive stress is experienced in those conditions where one can't be active in one's response, such as the death of a loved one. For those experiencing this type of stress, we see decreased vaccine response because a strong immune response is required to build antibodies in reaction to a vaccine. We also see poor wound healing and poor surgical outcomes.

The key ingredient of passive stress is the perception of not having control. The perception of not having control causes the stress—regardless of whether one has control or not. If someone perceives that they have control, they won't experience this type of stress nor its negative effects on immunity. The following experiment is sure to clarify the impact of perception.

Researchers divided people into four groups and put them in separate rooms, with significantly loud noise close by. The first group had a lever to turn off the noise in their room. The second group had a lever but the lever didn't work. The third group had no noise (their room was insulated). The fourth group had the loud noise and no lever.

The NK cell activity (NK cells are type of cells that are critical to the immune system) went down in the fourth group participants, those with the loud noise but no lever. Others had no change in their NK cell activity, even those with the broken lever and with the perception of control. This demonstrates that by "feeling" that you have control over the situation, you can protect yourself from passive stress. Therefore, finding those aspects of a stressful situation that you have some control over and taking relevant actions are likely to give you relief, even if doing these things doesn't affect the situation itself.

In the case of the loss of a loved one, you won't be able to act on the situation itself, but finding something that you can do, such as helping others or volunteering for a cause that is relevant and meaningful, is likely to help you feel that you have some control and reduce the impact of stress.

Cancer

There are many studies that show links between stress and cancer. Even though they are not definitive and many are conducted on animals, there is still enough data to show that there is a relationship between the two.

Cancer cells are created from normal cells, when genes responsible for division and growth go awry. A healthy immune system is necessary to recognize and get rid of those cancerous cells before they turn into tumors and spread. We already discussed how stress affects immunity, and therefore it is easy to see how stress may affect cancer.

For cancer, research has shown that social stressors in particular are most dangerous. For example, some studies show a twofold increase in breast cancer risk after disruption of marriage, because of divorce, separation, or death of a spouse. Reaching out to positive social support could help to combat this aspect of stress.

Allergies

In 1970, it was estimated that only one in ten Americans had allergic disease. By the year 2000, that estimate went to one in three having an allergic disease. Allergies are due to a hyperactive immune system trying to fight something that isn't really a threat.

We mentioned earlier that stress decreases immunity. How do we explain then that stress causes allergies when allergies are due to a hyperactive immune system? That is because the stress hormones decrease immunity when they are released in large bursts. If, however, one is chronically stressed, and therefore experiences a low level of stress hormones at all times, this causes a deregulated immune system which over-responds at times and under-responds other times. Such a hyperactive immune system causes allergies.

Furthermore, when we are under stress, we are less able to detoxify allergens, and therefore our immune system has to mount a larger response to get rid of the allergen, which of course isn't effective and makes us feel miserable.

Stress and illness

Even though everyone experiences stress, not everyone is going to wind up with these diseases. People who have pre-existing vulnerabilities, such as genetic predisposition and other factors, are more likely to suffer from these diseases when they are exposed to severe burdens of stress. These same people may maintain normal health during normal stress conditions. Stress is one factor out of many other factors that can play into these diseases. However, stress is an important factor and one that we have some control over. Let us then continue to tackle stress and make your stress management toolbox even more effective.

Overcoming physical stress

For the most part, physical stress is brought on by subconscious effects through the involuntary nervous system, as I established earlier. The key to counteracting these harmful involuntary processes is to engage the voluntary nervous system to stop the involuntary response and consequently reduce the subsequent physical effects.

Try this. Take a deep breath in and imagine sucking the air all of the way down into your abdomen, and then slowly let it all the way out. Take another deep breath, but this time fill your chest and push your ribs out. Feel the spaces between your ribs expanding as you fill them with air. Do this two more times, slowly in and slowly out. Notice how you feel after this exercise.

I'm going to guess that you're feeling differently from how you were feeling before the exercise. This conscious way of breathing is "different" from the unconscious way that you were breathing before. This is exactly the point. You can't breathe involuntarily at the same time that you are breathing voluntarily. In a way, this is similar to what we mentioned earlier about thoughts. You cannot hold on to two contradictory thoughts at the same time.

If you are engaging the voluntary nervous system, this will override the involuntary one. If we focus our efforts on what we can control, we will stop the reactions we're having in the moment and train our bodies over time to react differently in the first place and not be so reactive. The following two exercises can help you do exactly this.

Progressive relaxation

When we are stressed and in the freeze response, not only are we more likely to hold our breath, but we also tense our muscles. Dr. Jacobsen, who was a physician back in the 1930s and who came up with progressive relaxation, noticed that the patterns in our muscles constantly vary from moment to moment—not just in visible ways, but on a smaller level based on how we're thinking. He noticed that if a patient imagines he is rowing a boat, there are measureable rhythmic patterns from the arms, shoulders, back, and

166

legs of the patient as he engages in this act of imagination. The movements are miniscule but still measurable.

It seems that our thoughts and response patterns, including the freeze response, are constantly engaging our muscles, without us even realizing it. I'm sure you have noticed sometimes that you tend to hold tension in certain areas. You may, for instance, notice that when you don't feel safe, your shoulders roll forward or you keep them hunched up towards your ears.

Often, we don't notice these responses until they get to the point of causing us pain. The tension in muscles around the nerves can lead to pain and decreased function. Muscles, fatigued from being held in tension, develop spasms. It is not the entire structure that develops spasms but, rather, segments of the muscle producing the familiar painful knots that are also known as trigger points.

This relation of stress and muscular tension is so strong that if you learn to get rid of the excessive muscular tension, you can decrease the intensity of stressful emotions. Just like how changing our emotions can change the way our body feels, changing the way our body feels can change how we feel emotionally. For example, you can put your shoulders back into a position of confidence and start feeling a little bit more confident. Take a deep breath, straighten your posture, and put your shoulders back and your chin up into a position of confidence. Notice how you feel.

The full method of progressive relaxation consists of three stages. The first stage, which I describe below, consists of learning how to relax all the muscles in your body. The second stage consists of training your muscles that are not participating in an activity to relax. Your arm muscles, for instance, may need to contract to keep your arms extended, but your shoulders don't need to be up by your ears. The third stage consists of noticing which muscles are strained during the day when stressful situations happen. The goal of this stage is to be able to relax these muscles at the moment when tension happens. For instance, you may notice that fear causes you to roll your shoulders forward. So as soon as you feel fear, you should push your shoulders back to counteract that response and therefore that emotion.

In addition to the stress management benefits mentioned above, the progressive relaxation exercise we are about to describe can also help you relax and fall asleep at times when you can't.

Close your eyes and get into a comfortable position. Take a deep breath slowly through your nose, and imagine the breath filling your body all of the way into your feet. Let your breath out slowly. Continue breathing and imagining the breath filling your body all the way into your feet. Keeping your eyes closed, picture your toes. Then tense all of your toes as much as you can. Curl and hold them for a few seconds, keeping them as tense as you possibly can. Then release the tension. Keep focusing on your toes. Notice the difference in sensation from when they were tense. Take a deep breath into your toes, allowing them to relax further.

Leaving your toes in a relaxed state, picture your feet. Without tensing your toes, attempt to curl your feet into a tense position. Hold them for a few seconds, keeping them as tense as you possibly can. Then release the tension. Notice the sensation and breathe further relaxation into your feet.

Leaving your feet and toes relaxed, move your attention to your calves. Repeat the same process as above. Tense and then relax. Continue repeating the same process for one set of muscles at a time, such as the thighs, the buttock, the stomach, the back, the shoulders, the neck, the arms, and even the face.

At the end of the exercise, if you still notice tension anywhere in your body, try to relax it and imagine breathing into it. Feel the relaxation. Allow your body to stay relaxed. Finally, open your eyes, and slowly come back to a normal state, enjoying a whole new way of being.

Breathing exercise

Most of us are used to shallow breathing, using only a small percentage of our lung capacities. We need to do something to increase our lungs' abilities and get more of the benefits that deep breathing can give us.

Correct breathing purifies the blood, provides more energy, and even calms the mind and the body. In essence, breathing serves two purposes. It helps in transporting oxygen to various parts of the body, and it helps in the elimination of waste products. Shallow breathing fails to bring sufficient oxygen to the body and also fails to cleanse the body of all the waste products. The result is a lack of overall energy.

Having more oxygen clears the mind, rejuvenates the skin, and energizes your whole body. No wonder a yogi tends to have glowing skin and often looks far younger than his or her age. There are probably several reasons for that, but at least one of them is that they practice deep, yogic breathing. Yogic breathing practices engage and strengthen the ability of the voluntary nervous system and the capacity of the lungs. They also contribute to mindfulness, in that you're engaged in focusing on your breathing and therefore giving yourself a break from the mental contemplations that cause stress.

Get ready to relax. I am going to describe one type of yogic breathing exercise, which you can then use on your own. You close the right nostril with the right thumb and breath through the left nostril for a count of four. Then, you hold your breath for a count of eight. Finally, you breath out of the right nostril for a count of six and then breath into the right nostril for a count of four. Once again, you hold your breath for a count of eight. Then you breathe out of the left nostril for a count of six and then breathe into the left nostril for a count of four. And the cycle continues.

While it is beneficial to do so even for a few minutes, this is usually done for a longer count. The more you do it, the more you build up lung capacity.

Your Stress Management Mindmap

Start with the words "stress management" in the middle of your Mindmap. Add a branch for each area of your work and personal life in which you are experiencing unproductive stress. For each area, do the following:

Step 1: Rank it using the scale that we discussed earlier, in which one represents extreme stress and ten represents extreme happiness.

Step 2: Select an area that you would like to approach first. It is important to work on one area and make tangible progress in this area before you undertake additional areas. Otherwise, you may be creating stress instead of managing stress!

Step 3: Identify the stress management approach or technique that would be most applicable to this area. For instance, if you believe that it is your negative thoughts that are largely contributing to the situation, you may choose to apply the transforming your thoughts method discussed earlier. If, however, the situation relates to an interpersonal conflict, you may choose the Awareness Wheel. If the situation relates to having too many competing priorities and feeling overwhelmed as a result, you may then decide to tackle it using the Immediate Priorities Matrix, followed by setting expectations and negotiation.

Step 4: Put the stress management approach identified in step 3 to work. Step 4 is the core effort and where the rubber meets the road. This step consists of working through the situation and navigating through the difficult aspects of it to arrive at a resolution. Beware that it is an iterative process. The resolution may be several iterations away. Acknowledge every progress no matter how insignificant it may seem to be at the time. Appreciate that you are working through this process. By going through this process, you are building and strengthening your growth mindset. Also, keep in mind that the resolution may not necessarily consist of changing the situation. It may be changing your perception and replacing negative or distorted thoughts with more realistic ones. More often than not, a sound resolution is likely to involve both, some inner transformation combined with some external action. Action in this case will be based on awareness instead of reaction.

Step 5: Take action. This is the implementation step where you translate step 4 into action. Action brings the resolution to the real world and enables you to gather real data. Action cements the learning and brings about further growth. Being an iterative process, action may bring about further reflection and analysis, followed by further actions.

Once you make headway in this area of stress, you are ready to undertake another area. Leverage the experience and confidence that you built during this process to tackle the next area. The Stress Management Mindmap is your blueprint for a happier and more fulfilled life. Instead of working randomly on stress and finding yourself repeatedly encountering the same situations that you had previously addressed, this Mindmap enables you to build stress management capabilities. It becomes your evolving knowledgebase of stress management. This is rewiring your brain at its best.

The third phase of the leadership journey

The first phase of our leadership journey was focused on developing strengths—yours and others'. The second phase was about developing the growth mindset in which the emphasis was on embracing challenges and tackling weaknesses. My discussion of stress management marks the beginning of the third phase, which is about "transforming your thoughts." This phase is about going deeper into the growth mindset and starting to truly rewire your brain to create lasting changes. This is *leadership within*, which is a fundamental for leadership outside.

Behaviors, Behaviors, Behaviors

Create your Stress Management Mindmap and select one area to work on. As described above, the Mindmap is intended to help you examine the key areas in your life where you experience stress, decide which of the stress management tools best addresses each area, and then use those tools to identify the next action or actions that can take you from where you are to a slightly better place. There is no better time than now. Time yourself for fifteen minutes now and create your first draft of the Mindmap. Block fifteen to thirty minutes on your calendar to continue working on it within the next few days.

As you encounter stressful situations during your day, stop and reflect on what might be the underlying thought that is causing you stress. Replace this thought with a more realistic one. If this thought relates to an area that is not on your Mindmap, add the newly identified area to your Mindmap.

Experiment with one mindfulness practice each day. There are several possibilities, ranging from the three-minute mindfulness meditation described above to progressive relaxation, the awareness wheel, and the many forms of meditation, breathing, and stretching exercises that you may be familiar with.

Remember that mindfulness involves recognizing what is going on around you without reacting to it and therefore being less stressed and more productive. It starts with paying attention to what is happening now (present thoughts, body sensations, emotions) and then instead of passing judgment or reacting, simply accepting these thoughts, sensations, emotions, and letting them be. Mindfulness helps us stop being consumed by our unrealistic and sometimes compulsive thoughts, which are typically about the past or the future and how things and people should be and which can significantly diminish our effectiveness in and enjoyment of the present moment. Mindfulness also helps address background anxiety, which may be otherwise difficult to consciously pinpoint and transform.

Chapter 10: Mastering Nutrition for Peak Performance

Nutrition? Yes, nutrition! Nutrition impacts mental and physical well-being, focus, energy, mood, and ultimately performance; all important ingredients for successful leadership.

In this chapter, Deanna Moncrief, Principal of Benchmark Wellness, explores key principles related to nutrition and shows leaders how to simplify their approach to nutrition and reach peak performance. Ms. Moncrief has been in the wellness industry for the past twelve years and has broad expertise in the dynamics of wellness program management. With an advanced degree in Clinical Nutrition & Dietetics and a thriving private practice, she is closely in touch with what people want and need to be healthy. She has trained and guided companies across the U.S. in various stages of program deployment. She is a sought-after wellness expert and corporate trainer among local employers and national Fortune 500 companies. She helped many companies customize their wellness programs, to achieve high returns and high employee satisfaction.

Optimum Health

Optimum health means different things to different people. For some, this means simply being disease-free and not having to go to the doctor. For others, optimum health means having energy and sustained concentration, glowing skin, few signs of aging, and feeling good mentally, physically, emotionally, and spiritually. Whatever it means to you is correct; we only have ourselves to satisfy. However, there are some recognized habits of healthy people on which most doctors and nutritionists would agree.

Someone who eats enough of the right kinds of food in regular intervals, drinks enough fluids, does some form of regular physical activity, is able to manage stress, and enjoys a healthy immune system probably feels pretty healthy. These are great health benefits to strive for, since people who are healthy feel better, think better, and *get more accomplished.*

Maintaining good eating habits is one of the best ways to achieve optimum health, since we really are what we eat. Good nutrition can delay the onset of many age-related changes, such as cognitive decline, fine lines and wrinkles, and lifestyle-related diseases like type 2 diabetes and heart disease. In addition, maintaining a healthy weight keeps physiologic stress to a minimum. Physiologic stress, or stress at the cellular level, is caused in large part by free radicals which are a direct result of poor food choices, being overweight or obese[18], environmental pollutants, and mental stress. This can be a catch-22, because when we are stressed we often crave sugar and sodium, leading to poor food choices. Making sure good nutrition and eating habits are in place is essential to optimum health.

Good Nutrition

What Does "Good Nutrition" Really Mean?

We really are what we eat, and what we drink is important too. Diet is central to how we feel. For example, what is our body language saying? Do we feel well? Do we look well? Do we have low energy at certain times during the day that affects our participation in important events? Are we able to focus on projects, tasks, or other people in engaging ways?

Good nutrition ensures an adequate balance of nutrients every day. When we eat poorly, we get too much of the wrong chemicals and not enough of the right ones in our bodies; these are the vitamins, minerals, and phytonutrients that everyone needs to stay well.

Good nutrition will:

- Ensure you get all the nutrients you need for a healthy body.

- Help you feel more energized—healthy foods are less likely to result in the energy slump that often happens after consuming high-sugar and high-fat foods.

- Help to regulate metabolism for weight control.

- Help to prevent and even reverse some diseases.

---

[18] The definition of overweight is a body mass index (BMI) of >25, and obese is a BMI of >30.

- Take the guesswork out of preventing disease because much of the prevention you need is in what you eat.

Good Food, Bad Food

These terms, "good food" and "bad food" are used commonly among the general public, but nutritionists are reluctant to follow suit. We prefer to say that there are "healthy foods" and "unhealthy foods" instead. Different foods have such different characteristics of flavor, texture, smell, cultural significance, emotional attachment, and health benefits that it would be irresponsible to label a food as "bad" when it might in fact be important to someone else.

There is a wide spectrum of food attributes when it comes to nutrition. Some are calorie dense and are useful for those needing extra energy. Other foods are high in certain nutrients that would be harmful for some people. What's important is for everyone to decide what foods to eat and what nutrition habits to maintain so that optimum health is achieved. Generally, however, there are important things to consider when making personal decisions about diet quality.

Healthy Foods and Habits Improve Your Health and Productivity

Maintain healthy food habits and have:

- Stable energy levels
- Good digestion
- Weight maintenance or weight loss
- Reduced risk of chronic disease
- Positive attitude
- Stable mood
- Mental focus

Getting to—and maintaining—optimum health is a matter of choice. Every time we eat something, we are making a choice to put the food or drink into our bodies. Much of the time we do this without much thought at all; they are habits. Food-related habits include eating while driving, eating in front of the television or computer, eating from the same candy jar in the break room, or going through the drive-through every day after work. Habits will also include things like how often you eat, whether or not you skip breakfast, drink enough water, or eat your vegetables.

Moving to better food choices and habits takes effort. As adults, we have a lifetime of food preferences behind us that play a role in our habits today. Some of those habits may or may not be healthy. The good news is that when someone changes his or her diet in positive ways, it takes just four days for that person to start feeling markedly better. Four days is easy to maintain a change and then evaluate whether or not it can be incorporated permanently.

The important thing to remember is to make one change at a time, whether it be trading diet cola for plain water or eating a large salad with lean protein for lunch instead of the usual cheeseburger. Gradual, consistent, positive changes will pay off in terms of how you feel, think, work, play, and age.

Unhealthy Foods and Habits Risk Your Health and Productivity

Maintain unhealthy food habits and risk having:

- Inflammatory diseases
- Digestive disorders
- Overweight and obesity
- Weakened immune system
- Depression and unstable mood
- Cognitive decline and productivity loss

What you eat affects things like your body's level of inflammation, which, if chronic, can lead to pain, as well as the onset of autoimmune disorders like arthritis, lupus, or fibromyalgia, heart disease, stroke, or digestive disorders like ulcers, Crohn's Disease and Ulcerative Colitis. A depressed immune system is also a common side effect of poor nutrition, which allows oxidation of tissues and high amounts of circulating free radicals. This can also lead to mood instability, depression, and attention deficit or what is sometimes called "brain fog."

One important food habit that affects how you feel is how often you eat. Do you skip breakfast or wait until mid-morning to eat your first meal of the day? Do you work through lunch because you're too busy? Do you eat in the car or right before bed? Food frequency is an important factor to consider because it affects energy balance, which is the supply of calories being taken in relative to the calories expended. The type of food you choose is one side of the coin; how and when you eat is the other.

Nutrient Density

Foods containing the most nutritional value with the least amount of calories are considered *nutrient dense.* Nutrient-dense foods contain few calories and are rich in nutrients such as protein, carbohydrates, fats, vitamins and/or minerals. These foods are high quality and generally are minimally processed.

Foods containing high levels of calories per serving and little other nutritional value are considered calorie-dense foods. Although some may be sources of nutrients, others contain "empty calories."

Let's look at an example:

	1 slice of whole grain bread	½ bagel
Calories	80 calories	121 calories
Carbohydrates	15g	27g
Fiber	3g	1g
Fat	0.5g	1g
Protein	4g	1g

The slice of whole grain bread is more nutrient dense than the bagel, while the bagel is more calorie dense. The better choice would be the bread because it offers more bang for your nutritional buck. Food choices that are nutrient dense should comprise the bulk of a healthy diet.

The #1 Diet Rule: Stay Close to the Source

It may sound impossible, but there is a single rule for healthy eating! *Stay Close to the Source*.

Each time a food is chosen, decide how close to—or how far from—the source it is. In the above example, the apple is as close to the source as possible. Nothing has been added or removed from the apple, and it is in the same form as when it was hanging from the tree.

Applesauce is made from apples that have been processed, but nothing has been added (ideally, such as sugars) and only a small portion has been removed: the core and the skin. Unsweetened "natural" applesauce still contains the fiber originally found in the apple flesh.

Apple juice is also made from apples that have been processed, but even more has been done to them: the core and skin were removed, and the liquid has been separated from the flesh, also removing the fiber. Many apple juice products have added sugars, although even without added sugars the juice itself is simply the fruit sugar plus water. Apple juice is far from the source.

Further still is Apple Jacks cereal. While this product contains small pieces of real, dehydrated apples, so much has been done to this food that it no longer resembles an apple at all.

Applying this rule to everything you eat can have a huge impact on the quality of your diet. You can use the "apple/Apple Jacks" example for many foods and beverages.

Higher Quality/Close to the Source	Lower Quality/Far from the Source
Onions	Onion rings
Potatoes	Potato chips, French fries
Brown rice	White rice
Raw carrots	Carrot cake
Milk	Ice cream
Pure water	Sprite Zero
100% Whole wheat bread	"Wheat" bread
Raw honey, agave syrup, stevia	Sugar substitutes
Nutrient-dense whole foods	Energy bars

Simply, by eating foods closest to their natural state as possible, you'll be on the right track to optimal nutrition and optimal health.

Nutrients

Carbohydrates

The merits of carbohydrates have been debated for decades. In the 1980s the high-carb diet was considered healthy. In the 1990s the low-carb diet was trendy, and now we're back in balance.

Carbohydrates are the main source of energy in our diet, since they provide the power source for energy production in our cells. Carbohydrates get broken down into sugars before they're absorbed into the bloodstream and become *blood glucose.* Glucose is the preferred fuel for our brain (protein and fat can be used for energy, and the by-products from their metabolism can be used by the brain in the absence of glucose, but only at a reduced capacity). Our muscles also use glucose for fuel, whether they be your leg muscles for walking or running or your heart muscle, arguably the most important muscle in the body. It's best to choose high-fiber carbohydrates to slow down the rate at which they are absorbed, providing you with long-lasting energy.

Like protein and fat, carbohydrates provide essential nutrients but only if they are whole and unrefined. Carbohydrates can be complex (whole and unrefined) or simple (refined), and the complex varieties provide fiber that slows down their conversion to sugars and subsequent absorption. This is preferred because rapid absorption of sugar into the bloodstream and sudden rise of blood glucose can have deleterious effects, such as immune system suppression, headaches, irritability, anxiety, fatigue, and an increase in risk for type 2 diabetes and heart disease.

Simple Carbohydrates and Blood Glucose

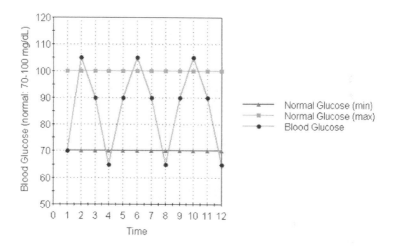

Which carbohydrates are eaten can have a definite impact on your waistline as well. When simple, refined carbohydrates are eaten and there is a rapid rise of glucose in the blood, the blood glucose will also fall rapidly. This "crash" can lead to increased carbohydrate cravings that can be satisfied with anything refined, such as hard candy, doughnuts, or potato chips. The repeated rise and fall of blood sugar, shown in the chart above, is a sure-fire way to gain weight; with each sugar "peak," a hormonal cascade is triggered that results in fat storage. For weight management, this is why a stable blood sugar level achieved by eating only whole, complex carbohydrates, is important.

For optimum health and sustained energy we need about 60% of calories from carbohydrates. Most should come from fruits, vegetables, whole grains, beans and legumes, which contain high amounts of nutrients and fiber. Very few calories should come from refined grains, white flours, refined sugars, and foods made with them, such as cakes, cookies, ice cream, doughnuts, tortillas, white rice, and many breakfast cereals.

Too many simple carbohydrates in the diet can impact your health, mood, and productivity by causing erratic changes in your brain that leave you feeling tired and depressed. Additionally, a high-sugar diet can increase the formation of compounds that accelerate aging. These chemicals, "advanced glycosylation end products," can create free radicals, known to increase the rate at which human cells age.

Here are some healthy carbohydrate foods:

Beans and legumes. These high-fiber nutrition jewels are slowly digested, and their carbohydrates are released into the bloodstream slowly, stabilizing blood sugar and leaving you feeling satisfied long after you've eaten. Beans also contain folate, a B-vitamin that humans cannot synthesize, so it must be supplied through the diet. Symptoms of low-folate status include diarrhea, headaches, heart palpitations, irritability, mental confusion, forgetfulness, and depression. Without adequate folate, a normally present amino acid called homocysteine can accumulate in the blood, increasing the risk of heart disease and stroke, and some recent studies suggest a low-folate/high-homocysteine combination can lead to an increased risk of cancer.

Brown rice. Did you know that brown rice is the same as white rice, but white rice is the refined form of brown rice after its "good stuff" has been removed? This "good stuff" includes two of the three parts of any grain: the bran, the germ, and the endosperm. The bran is the hard coating that protects the grain and provides fiber; the germ is a small but important part that provides protein and healthy fats, and the endosperm is the large, starch-filled portion of the grain that provides food energy (carbohydrate) for the plant. Eating brown rice ensures a whole, close-to-the-source food that is loaded with B-vitamins and a gradual release of sugar into the bloodstream.

Fruits. Fruits are a wonderful way to add color and sweetness while maintaining a close-to-the-source diet. Fruits have fiber, vitamins, and antioxidants that help prevent the outward signs of aging by keeping skin firm and glowing; they also help prevent internal aging processes, such as cancer development. Fresh fruits should be eaten in season and grown locally when possible. Frozen fruits are equally as nutritious since they are often flash-frozen in the field, reducing nutrient depletion that happens during shipment and storage of fresh fruits grown at a geographic distance. Beware of canned fruits and fruit juices (even 100% juices), since they are often higher in sugar.

Vegetables. Fresh vegetables grown close to home and organically are best, and frozen veggies are also good for the same reasons as frozen fruits. Dark green, leafy vegetables are superior choices since they are highest in nutrients like folate, fiber, and B-vitamins. Fresh vegetable juices are good choices as well, since they are often lower in sugar than fruit juices.

Sweet potatoes, winter squash, and other starchy vegetables. Although higher in starch, these vegetables are full of nutrients and fiber. Sweet potatoes, winter squash like butternut, acorn, and kabocha, and other starchy vegetables like carrots and yams contain beta-carotene, which is converted to vitamin A in the body. Beta-carotene helps repair the body's tissues and helps to protect your skin against sun damage.

Other whole grains. Unrefined, whole grains with all three of their "parts" (bran, germ and endosperm) are ideal carbohydrates because of their fiber content. They are also high in fiber and contain some protein, slowing down the absorption of sugars and subsequent conversion to blood glucose. Whole grains are also high in B-vitamins and include sources like quinoa (pronounced keen-wa), millet, amaranth, whole wheat, corn, and oats.

The Takeaway:

Eat These Close-To-the-Source Foods	Not These Far-From-the-Source Foods
Fruits	Soda
Vegetables	Fried foods
Beans	Refined flour and sugar
	Baked goods
Legumes	Sugar cereals
Starchy vegetables	Candy
Whole grains	White rice

Fiber

Current estimates suggest that Americans eat about 9 grams of fiber a day if that. Fiber is found in fruits, vegetables, grains, some nuts, and legumes and is a compound in carbohydrates that is not digestible since humans don't have the enzymes to break it down. Animal products like milk, meat, and cheese contain no fiber.

Fiber is important for good health because it acts like a broom in that it sweeps out both the small and large intestine, carrying with it things like cholesterol molecules (which is why fiber is said to lower cholesterol) and even some toxins, out of the body. The World Health Organization suggests that each person consume 30-40 grams of fiber a day.

As previously mentioned, fiber is helpful for slowing down the absorption of carbohydrates into the bloodstream, thereby keeping blood glucose relatively stable. This is important for disease risk reduction, weight management, energy and mood regulation, as well as general well-being.

Protein

Dietary protein is essential, meaning we can't get along without it. Proteins are made up of amino acids, building blocks necessary for the growth and repair for our cells, organs, and tissues. They are also used to create hormones, enzymes, and antibodies to strengthen our immune system. There are thousands of processes that keep you healthy every day, and the amino acids found in protein are required for most of them.

Most adults need about 3 to 5 ounces of protein at each meal, about the size of a deck of cards. Another way to calculate protein needs is by getting 15% of your calories from high-quality protein. Eating protein at each meal does a few things: Dietary protein helps to turn off the hunger mechanism, something carbohydrates can't do; by eating protein at each meal you're supplying a constant source of amino acids to your body all day; protein slows down the absorption of carbohydrates and subsequent conversion to blood glucose, keeping energy levels stable.

The best proteins include beans and legumes, poultry (without skin), fish, seafood, lean meats, eggs, and low- or non-fat dairy products like cottage cheese, yogurt, and milk. Great vegetarian sources include soy products, nuts and nut butters (without added sugar), beans, legumes, and low- or non-fat dairy products. A meatless, soy-free protein product called quorn is low in fat, high in protein, and low in sodium. It also contains no cholesterol. Quorn is made from all-natural ingredients, like eggs, and comes in chicken-like patties, nuggets, or "grounds" that look like ground beef.

Low-quality proteins include high-fat animal proteins like marbled beef or high-fat ground beef, lamb, dairy products with more than 1% fat, grilled meats, and cured meats. The quality of these protein sources is considered low because of the nutritional tradeoff: For each gram of protein, these foods also contain high amounts of fat, high amounts of dangerous chemicals, or both.

Animal meats, when heated to high temperatures such as is common in grilling, lead to the formation of chemicals that have been found to damage cellular DNA, which may increase the risk of cancer. These substances include heterocyclic amines (HCAs) and polycyclic aromatic hydrocarbons (PAHs). HCAs are formed when amino acids in animal meats, sugars, and creatine (a substance found in muscle meats) react at high temperatures. This reaction is what causes "grill marks" or charring. PAHs are formed when fat and juices from meats grilled over an open fire drip down, causing flames. The flames contain PAHs that adhere to the surface of the

186

meat; smoking of meats also causes the formation of PAHs. PAHs are also found in cigarette smoke and car exhaust fumes.

Cured meats are far-from-the-source proteins because they have been processed and much has been added to them. In particular, nitrates and nitrites have been added to foods like bacon, sausage, pepperoni sticks, and beef jerky to retard the growth of harmful bacteria. When in contact with stomach acid, these nitrates and nitrites form nitrosamines, which have been shown to cause cancer in humans. These compounds have also been shown to damage blood vessels and thereby increase the risk of heart disease, as well as negatively influence the way blood glucose is regulated, possibly increasing risk of type 2 diabetes.

Choose whole, close-to-the-source, unprocessed protein sources as often as possible. When you'd like to indulge in a grilled burger or some bacon with your eggs, be sure to load up on fruits and vegetables to add some powerful, protective compounds to the mix.

The Takeaway:

Eat These Close-To-the-Source Foods	Not These Far-From-the-Source Foods
Lean meats	Sausage
Poultry without skin	Grilled meats with charring
Beans and legumes; soy	Bacon
Nut butters with no sugar added	Hot dogs
Low-fat dairy products	Beef jerky
Eggs	Nut butters with sugar added

Fats

Fat, like protein and carbohydrate, is an essential nutrient, meaning we need it to survive and be healthy. Fats cushion our organs, keep our body temperature at a normal 98.6°F, and are a concentrated source of energy. Fats play a role in hormone formation, as well as regulate the immune system. They are a necessary nutrient for the absorption of fat-soluble vitamins, such as vitamin A, vitamin D, and vitamin E.

Fats affect the formation of substances called *eicosanoids* that control inflammation in the tissues. Healthy fats promote the formation of helpful eicosanoids that decrease inflammation. On the other hand, inflammation is predominant with diets that are high in unhealthy fats. High levels of inflammation are associated with depressed immunity, increased pain, menstrual cramps, headaches, and heart disease.

Some guidelines suggest a fat budget of 30% of calories from fat, but recent recommendations are lower at 20-25% of calories from fat. The type of fat consumed is just as important as the overall quantity; it is critical to eat mostly unsaturated fats, keep saturated fats to a minimum, and maintain a balance between omega-3 and omega-6 fats.

Healthy, unsaturated fats come from plant and fish sources. These include olives, olive oil, nuts, avocados, flax and other seeds, salmon, mackerel and tuna. Saturated fats come from animal products like beef, poultry, lamb, pork, whole-milk dairy products, cheese, butter, and two plant sources: palm kernel oil and coconut oil. Saturated fats are more likely to be stored as body fat, while unsaturated fats are more readily used as energy and have other healthful benefits.

Unsaturated fats from plant and fish sources keep us healthy at the cellular level. They are used by the brain to maintain cognition and mood and by our skin to maintain elasticity and suppleness. Their high concentration of omega-3 fats helps to reduce the risk of age-related cognitive decline and dementia. These beneficial omega-3 fats are found in fish oil, flax oil, and walnuts.

Excess consumption of omega-6 fats relative to omega-3 fats has been linked to inflammation and various disease states, especially when combined with environmental and dietary pollutants, cigarette smoke, and second-hand smoke. Omega-6 fats are found in some plant oils, such as corn, safflower, sunflower, soy, and cottonseed. To maintain a healthy ratio of omega-3 to omega-6 fats, see *How to Change Your Oil,* below.

Trans fat is yet another type of fat that should be strictly limited in the diet. Trans fat occurs naturally in minute amounts in meat and dairy products but is largely found in the food supply as a result of processing. Food manufacturers begin with unsaturated oil and convert it into a more shelf-stable fat that helps foods stay flaky or crispy longer. This process is called *hydrogenation*. These resulting trans fats become "saturated fats" for all intents and purposes, and they are treated as such by the body. Trans fats also increase the "bad" LDL cholesterol and triglycerides, the fat droplets in blood causing it to become "sticky." Because trans fats are found largely in processed, packaged foods that are far from the source, they are easy to identify and limit in your diet. In fact, nutrition labels must list the amount of trans fat, so read those labels and limit yourself to no more than 2 grams per day.

How to Change Your Oil	
Decrease Saturated Fats: *Butter, cocoa butter, palm kernel oil, animal fats (beef, chicken, lamb, pork, turkey, whole-milk and more than 2% fat dairy products)*	**Increase Unsaturated Fats (within your 20-25% fat calorie budget):** *Fish, fish oil, flax oil, walnuts, avocados, olive oil, macadamia nut oil, canola oil*
Decrease Omega-6 Fats: *Corn oil, safflower oil, sunflower oil, soy oil, cottonseed oil.*	**Increase Omega-3 Fats:** *Free-range chicken eggs, kiwi, salmon, mackerel, halibut, flax seed, chia seed, kelp*
Avoid Trans-Fats! *Fats found in margarines and spreads, palm oil, hydrogenated and partially-hydrogenated vegetable oils, processed foods, crackers, ramen noodles, cake mixes, frozen foods, many peanut butters, fast foods, and fried foods*	

Saturated fats are ok to eat sometimes, but we really need to limit them to less than 10% of our total calories. Not only do saturated fats clog arteries and become very stubborn to burn off, they can negatively influence mood, focus, and productivity.

When you eat the right fats, you'll have greater immunity, with less inflammation, and you'll feel better and have optimal health. This will make you more able to work smarter, feel better, and enjoy life.

Water: The Other Nutrient

By and large, many adults are chronically dehydrated. We don't drink enough water! Many beverages we *do* drink (coffee, tea, and sodas) act as diuretics, meaning they increase urination, thus tipping the scales toward dehydration. In addition, many soups contain high amounts of sodium, so after a lunch of clam chowder, ramen, pho, or even some miso soups, we spend our afternoons retaining so much water that we feel thirsty. Even as our bodies hold onto excess water in an attempt to dilute the concentration of sodium, we are technically dehydrated; water can't get into our cells, and this affects our focus and energy levels drastically.

Water helps flush out metabolites, waste products, and toxins from the body, and dehydration will compromise this process. How much water is enough per day? The general recommendation for adults is eight 8-ounce glasses per day, or 64 ounces. Some may find it difficult to keep track of the number of ounces they are drinking, so experts suggest an easier way to make sure you're properly hydrated: drink enough water so that your urine is clear to pale yellow (dark urine may be a sign of dehydration).

Nature's Pharmacy

Not exactly nutrients, phytochemicals ("fight-o-chemicals") help to reverse damage from low quality diets, stress, and environmental pollutants and help protect against disease. Phytochemicals include a wide variety of plant compounds that may affect human health. They are found in fruits, vegetables, whole grains, beans, legumes, nuts, seeds, and teas. While scientists have studied only a fraction of the thousands of phytochemicals that exist in nature, there are three worth mentioning.

Antioxidants. These phytochemicals can help to neutralize harmful molecules called free radicals that can damage DNA and may trigger cancer and other diseases. Antioxidants can also strengthen your immune system and possibly lower your risk for infection. Commonly known antioxidants include vitamin C, vitamin

E, and others, and they are found in teas, broccoli, cabbage, Brussels sprouts, grapes, radishes, cauliflower, apples, red wine, raspberries, blackberries, cranberries, strawberries, and walnuts.

Natural Food Colors. Carotenoids are the natural compounds that make foods orange, such as apricots, yams, cantaloupe, carrots, mangos, and some squash. Lutein and zeaxanthin are carotenoids that give plants their yellows and greens, such as kale, nasturtiums (edible flowers), spinach, watercress, pistachio nuts, and kiwi. Lycopene gives the red color to tomatoes, red peppers, pink grapefruit, and watermelon. As a group, carotenoids are promoted as powerful anti-cancer agents.

The Stinkers. Another group of phytochemicals is called allyl sulfides. These compounds are responsible for the smell and flavor of garlic, onions, horseradish and wasabi and may stimulate enzymes that sequester and expel harmful chemicals from the body. Allyl sulfides have also been shown to help strengthen the immune system.

Nature has a lot to offer in terms of health benefits. Choose a wide variety of whole, close-to-the-source, colorful foods, and you'll be sure to get your share of disease-fighting goodness.

Food Dangers

Many food additives have been studied and linked to various diseases. Becoming informed about the additives in everyday foods can make for an easier shopping experience and healthier food for you. There are many useful food additives that prevent spoilage, increase shelf life, enhance flavor and texture, and add brilliant colors. However, many of these common additives are medically questionable and even harmful to human health:

Sodium nitrite. A preservative added most commonly to prevent botulism, it is often found in bacon, ham, hot dogs, sandwich meats, and smoked fish. In the presence of acid (such as in the human stomach), sodium nitrites are converted to nitrosamines, which are carcinogenic (can cause cancer).

BHA and BHT. Butylated hydroxyanisole and butylated hydroxytoluene are other preservatives added to foods like cereal, gum, potato chips, and vegetable oils. They have been identified as compounds "reasonably anticipated to be human carcinogens."

Monosodium glutamate (MSG). This flavor enhancer is often added to many prepared, canned, frozen, and processed foods. It has been linked to migraines, hormonal imbalances, and weight gain.

Artificial colorings. The FDA has banned many food colorings, but most can still be found in foods, beverages, candy, and gum. Red No. 40, Yellow No. 5 and Yellow No. 6, which make up 90 percent of the food dyes on the market in the United States, continue to concern many industry experts. Some consumer groups say that food dyes "are known to cause" child hyperactivity and even ADHD, while the food industry and the U.S. Food & Drug Administration recognize them as safe. The debate goes on.

Potassium bromate. This volume-enhancer is added to some breads and rolls to keep them soft and full, but it has cancer-causing properties that have prompted some states in America to actually require a label to that effect, most notably California. The U.S. Food & Drug Administration has urged bakers to stop using it voluntarily, as it has been shown to be a human carcinogen.

Avoiding food additives completely is almost impossible, but restricting these dangerous chemicals and focusing on eating fresh, natural, close-to-the-source foods will put you closer to optimal health, faster.

Behaviors, Behaviors, Behaviors

Achieving optimum health isn't always easy, especially if you have a long way to go. However, it doesn't have to be difficult either. The payoff is as good as the incremental benefits along the way. There are some key ingredients to keep in mind:

Educate yourself. Read information from reputable sources like universities, medical institutions, and nutrition professionals; learn what you can about disease prevention and healthy eating, and find solutions that work for you.

Stay motivated. Let your increased energy and healthy feelings motivate you to keep going.

Follow up. Let your physician know what changes you are making to your lifestyle. Keep following them, and when you make promises to yourself, see them through!

Commit. Make yourself and your health an absolute priority.

Seek support. Making lifelong changes can be difficult, but having supportive friends and family can make it easier. Let them know about the changes you are trying to make, and tell them what they can do to help you be successful.

When nutrition habits and food choices are unhealthy, people often suffer from fatigue, decreased mental capacity, irritability, stress, depression, and low productivity. Consider what *small, consistent changes* you can make to reverse these effects, and make them one at a time. Spend just four days on each one, and then evaluate whether you can adopt the change for good. If not, that's ok. Move on to the next one. What's important is to take action. Simply by taking steps in the right direction, you'll feel the health benefits and the motivation to continue.

Here's to your health!

Chapter 11: Leveraging Physical Activity and Boosting Engagement

Physical activity has a profound impact on wellness and productivity, in ways that are similar to the impact of nutrition. The combined effect of physical activity and healthy nutrition is what leaders need in order to muster the energy and endurance that are necessary to lead and inspire while maintaining great health, keeping stress well under control, and feeling good.

We all know by now that physical activity is good for one's health and that it is a key part of managing weight and keeping the heart, lungs, and other bodily systems in tip-top shape. However, there is more to it. There are some additional astonishing benefits to exercise, and there are significant challenges and obstacles that tend to get in the way of a regular exercise program. In this chapter, Jennifer Weland, Principal of Evolve Fitness & Coaching, covers the fundamentals of movement and exercise and explains how they can dramatically impact your life in so many ways, from making you more productive to boosting energy and stamina, to spurring creative thinking, to elevating your mood and even helping you sleep better, just to mention a few. In addition, having been in the corporate world throughout her career, Ms. Weland understands how difficult it can be to make room for exercise, and she addresses this issue head-on, sharing valuable insights into how to overcome the underlying challenges.

Ms. Weland works with clients locally in the San Francisco Bay Area and across the nation through her fitness and nutrition programs. She is certified as a Personal Trainer from the National Association of Sports Medicine (NASM), a Lifestyle & Weight Management Coach from the American Council on Exercise (ACE), and a TRX Instructor.

How Your Body Responds to Exercise

As soon as you *start* moving, your body knows that it needs to kick into gear to *keep* you moving. Your body responds in amazing ways to the demands you place on it.

Your brain releases a cocktail of hormones like norepinephrine, dopamine, and serotonin. Norepinephrine is part of your fight or flight response. It increases your heart rate, triggers the release of glucose from your body's energy stores, and increases blood flow to your muscles. Dopamine plays a major role in reward-motivated behavior and can make exercising light up your brain's pleasure center. Yes, that's part of why some people become addicted to exercising! Serotonin performs many functions, including regulating mood and appetite.

Your endocrine system—which releases chemicals and hormones to control physiological functions in your body—**starts sending messages via hormones to your cells and tissues,** telling your body to regulate temperature, heart rate, and blood pressure, to be alert and focus so you can work at a higher intensity, and to release stored carbohydrates in your body for energy.

Your metabolism fires up, burning available carbs to supply your body with energy to keep moving. Carbs are the easiest source of energy for your body, which is why they should be part of your diet. There are very heated debates about how many carbs you need and what kind you should be eating. What I want to convey here is that extremely low-carb diets can be problematic, especially for people who exercise frequently and at higher intensities.

Your muscles contract and relax, which causes your joints to move—when you're running, lifting a weight, doing a yoga pose, or whatever form of exercise you've chosen. You need more oxygen to supply your working muscles, so you start breathing faster to draw in more air. During peak exercise, your lungs can breathe up to twenty-five times their resting capacity per minute.

And your muscles and other tissues need more blood, so your heart pumps faster to provide it. When exercising vigorously, your heart can beat at double or more the average resting rate of seventy beats per minute. What's interesting is that the more you exercise, the more efficient your heart gets at pumping blood. So, your resting heart rate could lower quite a bit. For example, my resting heart rate is fifty-six beats per minute.

And with those adaptations come the benefits of exercise. Let's start with some important health benefits that make a huge difference in how you feel and can dramatically improve your quality of life and how long you live.

198

Health Benefits of Exercise

Your heart and lungs get stronger. The more you require of them to supply blood and oxygen as you exercise, the more efficient they get at doing that. A stronger heart reduces your risk of cardiovascular disease and stronger lungs give you more endurance and capacity for strenuous activity. So you can go harder and longer when you want to, without tiring so easily.

Your biometric markers improve. Have you ever heard the phrase, "Know your numbers?" Probably at work and related to your company's wellness program, if you have one. It's referring to your biometric numbers, also called your biometric markers. Those markers include:

- your blood pressure

- fasting glucose level

- cholesterol level

- triglycerides level

- body mass index (BMI)

These are important indicators of how healthy you are overall. Diet and exercise keep all of these in check—so your weight stays at an optimal level for your body, and your blood pressure, cholesterol and blood sugar stay within normal levels. The better your numbers, the lower your risk for chronic or serious conditions like heart disease, some types of cancer, stroke, and type 2 diabetes. And if your company offers a wellness program with incentives for good numbers, you could pay less for health insurance, which is a nice bonus!

And finally, exercise combined with a balanced diet can reduce your risk of developing type 2 diabetes by 50 to 60 percent, or reverse it if you already have diabetes.

Thirteen Other Surprising Benefits of Exercise

Beyond the fantastic health benefits of exercise, there are so many more advantages to talk about. Let's start with five that improve how you perform at work.

1. A sharper mind

Because you flood your brain with oxygen, hormones, and nutrients during exercise, you create the perfect environment to grow new brain cells and stimulate more of a protein called brain-derived neurotropic factor (or BDNF). Surges in BDNF may be the reason why adults who exercise regularly show sharper memory skills, higher concentration levels, more fluid thinking and reasoning, and greater problem-solving skills than sedentary adults. All things we'd like to have, right? That's not to say that inactive people don't grow new brain cells, because of course they do. But exercise is known to spark the creation of two or three times as many new hippocampal neurons. Your hippocampus is *the most vital part of your brain* for memory and learning. Exercise also triggers endorphins, which can help you prioritize better after your workout session.

2. Endurance

Being fit makes you able to keep at whatever you're doing for a longer period of time. You're less likely to get fatigued during the day, so you can be more productive when you're on the clock. And you have energy to spare when you're off the clock!

I don't know about you, but when I wasn't exercising regularly, and I was working a desk job, I would be a complete zombie when I got home from work. I was so tired I could barely muster up the energy to make dinner. Now that I exercise almost every day and stand up more when I'm working, I have a lot of energy left over when the workday is done that I can use doing fun things or spending quality time with friends and family.

3. Ability to focus

Exercising before doing something that will require a lot of focus helps you be at your peak when you do have to perform. That's because exercise can raise your focus for two or three hours afterward, according to Dr. John Ratey, author of *Spark: The Revolutionary New Science of Exercise and the Brain.* Sharper focus comes in handy if you have a big presentation, speaking engagement, or a really big meeting where you need to be on. Or if you're about to take on a task that requires a ton of focus—like working through a giant forecasting spreadsheet.

4. Creativity Boost

When we exercise, it's a chance to get out of our heads and allow our minds to just relax. It may sound counterproductive, but how many times have you felt a surge of creativity while your mind was occupied elsewhere doing an unrelated physical task? For example, washing dishes, chopping vegetables, mowing the lawn, or folding laundry. Two places I seem to get some of my best ideas are in the shower and when I'm in the hills hiking. What about you? Think about where you get your great ideas or feel creative. Where are you when that happens?

If you're feeling stuck or out of ideas, try doing something else, like going for a walk. It doesn't really matter what you do and how long you do it. The change of place and focus will help the ideas flow. And even a short bout of exercise produces long lengths of boosted creativity.

5. Better mood

I mentioned earlier that exercise leads to the release of serotonin and dopamine. Both work to put you in a better mood, give you energy, and motivate you.

When you're in a good mood, you are a much better problem-solver because you're more willing to explore out-of-the box ideas. Plus, you're more fun to work with—willing to listen to others' ideas, less impatient, and less likely to react rashly to what someone says or does. Your good mood can spill over at home, too. I'm sure your spouse, significant other, and children, if you have any, will appreciate your better mood when you get home from a long day.

These next benefits aren't necessarily work-related, but they have a big impact on your quality of life.

6. More lean muscle

Resistance (or strength) training adds lean muscle mass to your body. Why would you want to put on lean muscle? There are three really good reasons:

First, to slow down the natural loss of muscle tissue that happens as we age. When you hit age thirty, you start losing about a half-pound of muscle each year.

Second, to change your body composition—which is the ratio of lean mass to fat mass. The better the ratio, the healthier you are and the more lean and toned your body looks. A lower body fat percentage means you could uncover the four- or six-pack you thought you'd never see.

And third, to burn even more calories, since muscle burns way more calories per pound per hour than fat—6.5 calories per pound per hour versus only 1.2.

Stronger muscles are denser, more metabolically active and require more calories to feed and maintain. Which is good news for your metabolism. Depending on how long and how hard you exercise, your metabolism can actually stay elevated for up to twenty-four hours after your workout. It's a concept called "after-burn." You can up the after-burn affect by challenging yourself—like with an interval workout, lifting heavier weights or doing high-intensity activities. For example, an hour-long boot camp class that mixes functional exercise with plyometric bursts or high-intensity interval training circuits will keep you burning calories long after that sweat session is done.

7. Buzzing metabolism

A speedier metabolism is important at any age, but will become even more critical when you pass age forty, because that's when it naturally starts to slow down by about 3 percent per decade. That happens, in part, because of the gradual loss of lean muscle mass. So, the faster and more efficient you can make your metabolism, the more you can fight that natural slow down, reducing it pretty significantly.

8. Manage stress

Exercise helps you reduce and better manage stress by lowering the amount of cortisol your body makes. This is so important because I don't know of anyone who doesn't feel some stress every day. Too much stress—and the effect it has on your body—has some serious consequences.

I'm sure you've heard the term "fight or flight response." It's short hand for what happens in your body when it needs to deal with stressors. Three hormones—epinephrine (also known as adrenaline), norepinephrine, and cortisol work together to help your body deal with stressors and get you back into "pre-danger" mode. The problem is fight or flight response happens to *all* stressors because your body doesn't know the difference between the short-term survival stressors, like getting chased by a bear, and longer-term stressors, like the deadlines you're bombarded with at work, the traffic that drives you crazy, and just about everything else in our modern society. That means we're all dealing with the effects of stress all the time.

When stress is always present, your body can't get rid of the excess cortisol that builds up in your blood. It hangs around—sort of like the houseguest that won't leave—turning your young fat cells into mature fat cells that stay with you *forever*. That excess cortisol increases your cravings for high-fat, high-carb foods because they cause chemical releases in the brain that make you feel good and counteract the stress side effects. And that excess really messes with your mood, your concentration, and your creative thinking ability.

9. Healthy Back

Exercise strengthens your core—which consists of the "tire" of muscle around your spine that takes the pressure off your vertebral bones and discs and the nerves that generate pain. A stronger core means less back pain and less risk of postural issues, like rounded shoulders and forward-extending necks that are common for those of you who spend hours sitting at a desk or at a meeting table or wherever you are doing the majority of your computer work.

Next time you're in front of a mirror, turn to the side and check out your shoulders and neck. Are your shoulders looking a little rounded from being hunched at your desk? Is your neck extended forward from looking at the screen? These are both signs that you need to focus on strengthening your core and back and that you need to stretch regularly.

10. Immunity "kung fu"

The more you move, the less likely you are to get sick from the random cold or flu that's passed down from coworker to coworker or from your children's school or day care to you. Research shows that exercise likely creates a temporary rise in your immune cells. A University of Wisconsin–Madison study reported that people who exercise regularly see a 29 percent decrease in the frequency of colds. And in a large 2010 study, those who were active at least five days per week cut the length of their cold almost in half. In other research, people who exercised after getting a flu shot nearly doubled their immune response.

11. Calm under pressure

Physical activity boosts blood flow to the parts of the brain that keep you calm. I'm sure you can easily think of several situations at work or at home when remaining calm would have helped you navigate a tough situation or deal with someone who was really stressed out or angry or out of control. Or how staying calm would have helped you handle a crisis. A study in *Medicine & Science in Sports & Exercise* found that not only did people score lower on anxiety tests right after working out, but they also kept their cool thirty minutes later.

12. Younger looking skin

It turns out sweating is good for your skin too. Studies show that regular workouts increase overall circulation and the skin's natural ability to produce collagen—which your body needs to keep your skin looking plump and young as you get older. Some of your sweat evaporates to cool your body and the rest is reabsorbed into the skin, giving it a nicely hydrated look post-workout. So much better than the grayish pallor you get from being stuck indoors all day under fluorescent lighting, right?

13. Better sleep

Working out zaps stress and anxiety, and your body gets better at regulating its own temperature so you can sleep more peacefully. In a 2011 study, people who did a total of 150 minutes of moderate-intensity exercise per week were able to fall asleep faster and felt less tired during daylight hours. You may have heard or read somewhere that working out in the evening could mean trouble falling asleep. But only limited research suggests that late night physical activity hurts the quality of your sleep. So don't skip the workout if evening is the only time you can get it in.

How Much Exercise You Need to Reap the Benefits

After reading about all of those great benefits, I'm sure you're asking yourself, "How much and what kind of exercise do I need to get, then?"

The *2008 Physical Activity Guidelines for Americans,* published by the U.S. Department of Health and Human Services, recommend:

- 150 minutes weekly of moderate-intensity OR

- 75 minutes weekly of vigorous-intensity aerobic activity for adults.

When you work at a moderate-intensity, it means you're working hard enough to raise your heart rate and break a sweat. You should be able to talk but not be able to sing the words to your favorite song. Walking fast, riding a bike on even ground, or playing tennis should get you there.

Working out at a vigorous intensity means you're breathing hard and fast and your heart rate has gone up quite a bit. If you're working at this level, you won't be able to say more than a few words without stopping for a breath. Jogging, running, or riding a bike fast or on hills will do the trick.

Adults should also get two or more days per week of muscle-strengthening activities that work all major muscle groups. Muscle-strengthening activities can include lifting weights, doing exercises that use your body weight for resistance, heavy gardening, or yoga. You can do activities that strengthen your muscles on the same or different days that you do aerobic activity, whatever works best. Just keep in mind that muscle-strengthening activities don't count toward your aerobic activity total.

The health benefits only increase when you invest more time in being physically active. For example, increased endurance, strength and speed, positive changes to body composition, and an even more efficient metabolism.

So, Why Aren't You Exercising More?

I doubt there is anyone who would say that exercise isn't good for you and that we don't need to do it. So, why aren't we exercising as much as we know we should? We all have our reasons. Some are legitimate, like we're working late or we're nursing an injury. But often we just talk ourselves out of it. And it's probably with one of these excuses:

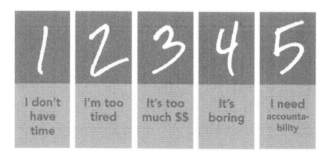

Let's dig into these a little bit and flip the script on them so they are no longer excuses for not exercising.

I don't have time

There is a good reason why "I don't have time" is the number one excuse. We're all busy trying to manage life's demands and a never-ending to-do list. *But the time IS there.* If you work fifty hours a week and sleep around seven hours (or less for many of us), that leaves at least sixty-two to sixty-nine hours a week for other stuff like exercise.

Three easy strategies I share with my clients—and that I practice myself—to fit in exercise every week are:

1. Scheduling your workouts in your calendar just like any other appointment and not letting other things push it aside.

2. Working out in the morning when you typically have the fewest conflicts. And as an added bonus for getting it done first thing, you get the benefit of an all-day boost in mood and energy. Plus, you get more time to enjoy the after-burn effect on your metabolism.

3. Finding ways to cut back on time-suck activities, like watching TV or logging on to social sites. There are loads of studies showing the average American spends about five hours a day watching TV. Thinking about your habits, how much time do you spend on those activities? I'm sure you could cut back by thirty to forty-five minutes a few times per week. If you did, voila! There's plenty of time to fit in your workouts.

What would your week look like if you exercised enough to meet the recommended minimums? You might be thinking that 150 minutes (or 75 minutes) of aerobic activity plus two strength days each week sounds like a lot. But it really isn't if you break it down this way:

Sun	Mon	Tues	Wed	Thurs	Fri	Sat
30 minute walk or bike ride	30 minutes strength	40 minute walk or bike ride	40 minute walk or bike ride	30 minutes strength	40 minute walk or bike ride	60 minute yoga class or rest

This sample plan adds up to just about four hours. Out of the about 119 hours you are awake during the week, that's only 3% of your time!

Sun	Mon	Tues	Wed	Thurs	Fri	Sat
Rest	30 minutes strength	35 minute run or hike in the hills	Rest	30 minutes strength	40 bike ride in the hills	Rest

And if you're working out at a vigorous intensity, that commitment gets even smaller. Seventy-five minutes of vigorous intensity activity and two days of strength training add up to only two and a half hours per week. You have two and a half hours a week you can spend on your health and well-being, right?

No energy

You are not tired at the end of the day because you get too much exercise. You're tired because you don't get enough exercise. Like most people, you are probably mentally, emotionally, and physically drained from being sedentary. Study after study shows that people are more productive and happier—on less sleep—when they are fit. Unless you're sick, you have enough energy to exercise—you just need to tap into it.

Waiting until you feel like doing something you don't want to do means you probably won't do it. Instead, commit to ten minutes of exercise to shake off your sluggishness. You'll most likely feel energized and ready to keep going. If not, stop there and get back on track tomorrow. At least you will have done something that counts toward your weekly goal. Shifting your workouts to the morning may also help.

It's too expensive

You don't need a gym membership to get in great workouts. Being a trainer, you'd think I practically live at the gym. But I don't even have a membership. I do my workouts in the same gym I train clients in only once a week so I can use some of the equipment. The rest of the time, I exercise at home or outside with minimal equipment like dumb bells, a stability ball, a medicine ball, and a few kettle bells. Add in body weight exercises, and you've got everything you need for a total body workout that burns a ton of calories.

There are a ton of free workout routines on the web, including on my website at **www.evolvefitnessandcoaching.com**, that require minimal to no equipment. I also created three custom "do anywhere" workout routines for you that can be accessed using a special link, www.evolvefitnessandcoaching.com/movemore. You can also download a 30-Day Challenge that provides a selection of activities to help you get more movement in at work and at home. Choose one each day. You will also find at my website health and fitness tips, recipes, workouts, and other resources.

It's boring

Boredom is a big problem when it comes to exercise. When you're bored, you either skip the workout, or you tend to try to make the time go faster by zoning out and flipping through a magazine or just letting your mind wander. Neither is good.

It's probably time for something new. Find five different workouts that you want to try, such as trail running, boot camp in the park, Zumba, or a TRX suspension training class at the gym. Just like dating, if you put yourself out there and try new things, you're bound to find something you love and that you'll want to stick with.

One other suggestion to break through a wall of boredom is by turning your workout into a challenge.

- Can you build leg strength by changing your bike route to include a few hills?

- Or can you push your aerobic potential by jogging and/or running/sprinting in intervals during your walk?

- Can you add more reps or more weight to your strength routine to work your muscles to fatigue?

You need accountability

Some of us need help following through. I hear this a lot. If you need some help staying accountable for working out, you could:

1. **Get a workout buddy**. It's hard to blow something off when someone is expecting you to show up. And you have someone to share the experience with and who can push you to keep going beyond what you might do on your own.

2. **Get a trainer**. Find a professional who will guide your efforts, motivate you, and hold you accountable for showing up and giving it your best effort. Look for a trainer you like but who's a real motivator—someone who you'll want to work hard for and you will like hearing praise from.

3. Or, **use technology to connect with others all over the country**. Check out apps like Fitocracy, which is similar to Facebook for fitness enthusiasts. You earn points for workouts, and you get compliments on your progress with messages like "How does it feel to be awesome?" You can also track the progress of other people, earn badges, and give and get props.

Sitting Disease

So, now you know all about the benefits of regular exercise and how much you need to get in each week. I could stop right here, but there's a big *Uh oh* that is preventing most of us from getting those benefits. Most of us are suffering from a serious condition called sitting disease that is killing our productivity and our bodies.

Spending hours on end in a chair, in the car, on the bus or train, on the couch, and in bed isn't just murder on your back. It can literally kill you. This isn't breaking news. In 2011, there was a pretty powerful infographic that made the rounds. You can see the infographic online—just Google the words "sitting too much infographic" to find it. It explains in a simple—yet really compelling way—how sitting wrecks your body and makes you fat.

If you ask most regular exercisers who sit for long periods, they'd probably tell you they're exempt from sitting disease because they exercise. Unfortunately, they are wrong. Exercise is only part of the prescription to combat the effects of sitting disease.

As a society, we are more sedentary than ever.

- Less than two in ten Americans gets even the recommended amount of exercise we just talked about. Even worse, 40 percent of Americans say they never exercise.

- We're awake about sixteen or seventeen hours each day. But according to the *Scandinavian Journal of Medicine & Science in Sport*, our muscles are inactive about 72 percent of that time—or eleven and a half hours per day—even if you're exercising.

How is that even possible? I'll tell you.

- If you're like the average person, you clock almost fifty-five hours a week sitting—sitting in traffic, sitting in mass transit, sitting at your desk, around the meeting table, sitting on the couch, laying in bed.

- We watch about five hours of television a day, as I mentioned before—all while sitting or lying down.

- And, according to a recent survey of 1,300 women by *Shape Magazine* and SheKnows.com, 47 percent of respondents spent two to five hours on social media each day.

With stats like those, it can't be a surprise that sitting disease is the smoking of our generation.

Your Body on Sitting

I want you to understand what happens to your body when you sit for long periods of time in the hope that it will prompt you to get up more often, stretch, breathe, and move around.

Your brain. The more you sit around, the more likely you are to fall prey to so-called senior moments. Your hippocampus—

remember, it's responsible for learning and memory—naturally deteriorates as you age. But the side effects of sitting too much, like obesity and diabetes, can speed that process up. And while sedentary people do grow new hippocampal neurons, exercise creates two or three times more.

Your butt. Eating too much isn't the only way you add unwanted junk to your trunk. A recent cell culture study found that when you sit for long periods of time, the weight your body puts on your fat cells actually encourages them to create twice as much fat—at a faster rate—as when you are standing. The fat that's created are triglycerides—the worst kind of chub. High triglyceride levels raise your risk of stroke.

Taking vanity into account here for just a second, too much sitting can lead to a little phenomenon I like to call "office chair ass." Your butt gets wider and flatter, like your office chair seat. And it becomes more cellulite ridden, giving it that dimpled appearance no one wants.

Your posture. Staying seated for hours at a time tightens your hip flexors and chest, and it weakens your core, which means a slumped posture and back pain. Back pain is the number one disability for those under age forty-five. In the United States alone, there is an expected thirty-one million people with lower back pain at any given time.

Tightened hip flexors and chest muscles and a weak core increase your risk for developing the postural issues we talked about earlier—rounded shoulders and forward-extending necks. People who suffer from these issues often have trouble performing daily tasks. And these issues are more likely to get worse as you age.

Your blood sugar. Every time you eat, your blood sugar spikes, and you get this huge four-hour crush of calorie-storing activity as your body goes through the normal process of digesting and metabolizing the nutrients in what you ate. Recent research shows that when otherwise healthy people halved the number of steps they took per day, their blood sugar spikes *increased* more than normal after each meal. And it didn't matter what type of food they ate—even if it was low on the glycemic index (which is a numerical scale used to indicate how fast and how high a particular food can raise our blood glucose level). These increased spikes are linked to a higher risk for type 2 diabetes.

Your breath. Something as simple as breathing can get bunged up by too much chair time. Our energy level depends in large part on our breath. Breathing deeply brings more oxygen into the body, increasing energy levels. The more you sit—and the worse your posture is while you are sitting—the more shallow your breaths become.

Take a second and pay attention to your breathing right now. I bet you it's pretty shallow and it's been some time since you took a deep, cleansing breath. Breathe deeply a few times right now to help restore your energy.

Your metabolism. Sitting expends almost no energy, because if you're sitting, your muscles are not contracting, except maybe to type or hold your phone to your ear or your iPad at reading level—small muscles and small movements. But the big muscles, like in your legs and back, are sitting there pretty quietly. When you are not moving your major muscles, your metabolism slows way down. Calorie burning drops to one per minute. Enzymes that help break down fat drop 90 percent.

Your sleep. When you're plopped in a chair or on the couch for hours, gravity and a lack of circulation can cause a buildup of fluid in your lower legs. After you get in bed at night, that extra fluid that built up migrates to the muscles and tissues of your neck and may force your throat to swell. A swollen throat makes it harder for you to draw in enough air, and you might even stop breathing for short periods during the night, which is a serious condition called sleep apnea. Not getting enough restorative sleep can leave you feeling like a zombie during the day.

Stop Sitting Disease in Its Tracks

The good news is that you don't have to suffer the effects of sitting disease. You can stop it in its tracks with a prescription of regular exercise PLUS more daily activity.

The *2008 Physical Activity Guidelines for Americans*, published by the U.S. Department of Health and Human Services, recommend the following amount of weekly exercise for adults:

- 150 minutes of weekly moderate-intensity **OR**

- 75 minutes of weekly vigorous-intensity aerobic activity **PLUS**

- Two or more days per week of muscle-strengthening activities that work all major muscle groups.

That amount adds up about four hours per week. Use the sample plan later in the chapter to help you fit it into your schedule. And remember, more vigorous-intensity activity shortens that time commitment to about two and a half hours.

Standing, walking, and moving more will not only help your back, shoulders, and neck, but it will also give you more energy, keep your metabolism stoked, and boost your productivity.

It doesn't have to be hard or take a ton of time. Here are six easy ways you can build more activity into your workday:

1. **Ask for a sit-to-stand desk** if your company supports it. If not, try setting your laptop on any stable surface that's high enough for you to be able to type comfortably (arms at right angles) and where your head is not looking too far down.

2. **Stand while talking on the phone or while in a long meeting.** It fires up leg and back muscles, which helps move fat and sugar in the blood and through the body.

3. **Replace desk chairs with stability balls**. Also a good option if the sit-to-stand desk is a no-go for you or you have a desktop computer.

4. **Take the stairs.** Climbing just two flights of stairs every day could result a loss of up to 6 pounds per year. Six flights a day could help you trim nearly 18 pounds.

5. **Ditch the email and instant messenger**. Walk over to your colleague and have conversations face-to-face. Think about the amount of emails you could cut out if you tried this tip!

6. **Hold a walking meeting with co-workers** instead of your usual conference room. Walking burns three to five times the calories that sitting does. And—as I mentioned earlier—it can help boost creativity. If you can, take the walking meeting outside in a non-busy area and get a little nature time or, as you've probably heard it referred to in many recent articles, *Vitamin N*.

Why is getting more *Vitamin N* important? Because holing up in an office all day under fluorescent lighting deprives you of two mental-health benefits:

- The first is Vitamin D, which your body produces in response to sunlight. Vitamin D helps protect against depression.

- The second is nature itself. We all need more of it because it soothes us on a subconscious level. In fact, in a recent study, brain scans showed that when people walked through parks, they were calmer and less frustrated than when they walked on busy city streets.

If you lead a team of people, help them out by encouraging these types of activities and supporting requests for sit-to-stand desks or stability balls to sit on. Make some of your meetings with staffers walking meetings so you set the example. Encourage more short breaks and getting people up out of their chairs. Consider a stretch or health moment before or after meetings.

Use these five ideas to get more activity outside of work:

1. If you take public transportation, always stand on the train or bus, and get off a stop or two earlier to squeeze in extra steps.

2. Stand while watching your kid's sports game or waiting at the doctor's office.

3. Park farther from the door when you go to the grocery store or the mall.

4. Bring groceries in one bag at a time. Or take things from one room to another in multiple trips.

5. Move or do exercises like squats and jumping jacks during TV commercial breaks. There's a routine available on my blog at http://evolvefitnessandcoaching.com/blog/.

Wrapping Up

We've covered a lot of information, so let's recap the key points I'd like you to take away:

- Your body responds to the demands you place on it when you move or exercise, and those adaptions deliver some fabulous benefits.

- Regular exercise gives you a stronger heart and lungs, reducing your risk of serious or chronic illnesses and preventing or reversing type 2 diabetes.

- There are so many other benefits to exercise beyond those for your health—like managing stress, boosting productivity and creative thinking, better sleep, and so much more.

- Even with all of these tremendous benefits, we're not moving nearly enough! We spend much more time watching television and on social media than we do moving. Sitting too much is one of the leading causes of back pain and postural issues, and it could, literally, kill us in the long run because of how your body responds to inactivity.

- You need to get at least the recommended minimums to get all of the benefits I discussed. Getting more than the minimum means even more benefits.

- Common excuses we tell ourselves about why we don't exercise more—like "no time" and "no energy"—can be overcome with the tips and strategies shared above.

- And finally, you need to move a lot more during the day to battle the side effects of sitting disease—simply exercising thirty minutes or so a day won't do it.

Your Next Steps

- Get out of the chair, out of the car, and off of the couch more often.

- Make a plan to build regular exercise into your schedule so you can reap all of the benefits, improving your health and your quality of life. Use the tips and suggestions here to help you make time and find activities you like, so you stick with it.

- Ask for a sit-to-stand desk or a stability ball so you spend less time stuck in an office chair.

- Check out the resources created just for our leadership program participants and book readers at: www.evolvefitnessandcoaching.com/movemore.

- Check out additional health and fitness tips, recipes, workouts, and resources at: www.evolvefitnessandcoaching.com.

- Download three custom "do anywhere" workouts and the 30-Day Challenge at: www.evolvefitnessandcoaching.com/movemore.

Your Wellness Mindmap

Start with the word "Wellness" in the middle of your Mindmap. Add a branch for areas of wellness that we discussed, including nutrition, exercise, the sitting disease, sleep, play time, relaxation time, and any other areas that you identify as important to your overall wellness. For each area, do the following:

Step 1: Add the aspects of this area that you would like to improve. For instance, in the exercise area, you may identify several aspects based on Ms. Weland's insights and recommendations above, such as adding seventy-five minutes of weekly moderate-intensity exercise to the activities that you are already doing. Another aspect may be to use the stairs instead of the elevator in order to fight the sitting disease.

Step 2: Select one aspect of one area that you would like to approach first. It is important to work on one area and make tangible progress in this area before you undertake additional areas.

Step 3: Identify the specific actions that you would like to take as a result. This is the step where you become very specific about what you are going to do and when. If you decided to add seventy-five minutes of weekly moderate-intensity exercise, in this step you would you identify what form of exercise and when. This is also the step where you reflect on potential obstacles and what you need to do to proactively address these obstacles. For more ideas, refer to Ms. Weland's five excuses and her techniques for addressing these excuses.

Step 4: Just do it, as Nike said. There is no way around this step. If you find yourself somehow finding your way around it, go back to step 3 and maybe try different actions, work further on the excuses and objections, or enlist the help of coach.

Step 5: Reap the benefits, and when you are ready, select another aspect of this wellness area. Then leverage your success to tackle the next area of your Wellness Mindmap.

The Fifth Speed Revisited

I defined the five elements of speed a while back as being physical, mental, strategic, emotional, and psychological. I indicated that psychological speed, the fifth speed, is about facing the fear. It consists of identifying the thoughts behind your deep-seated fears and shattering these thoughts, replacing them with more realistic and constructive ones, and therefore eradicating these fears and moving toward accomplishment and happiness at warp speed.

When we have a fear that is slowing us down and blocking us from reaching our most desired goals, the Cognitive-Behavioral Theory discussed earlier tells us that it is likely that there is an irrational thought behind the fear. Facing the fear would be identifying this thought, clearly pointing out the irrational aspects of this thought, and going after them. This means disputing them, disproving them, and transforming them. We covered a myriad of techniques that can help you accomplish exactly that. The awareness wheel, for instance, helps you uncover your interpretations and assumptions, become aware of your underlying feelings, and then get yourself unstuck. Instead of experiencing the freeze response to these thoughts and feelings, it enables you to move forward in clarifying your wants and identifying the actions that will move you toward these wants.

Similarly, the transforming your thoughts techniques from the stress management chapter enable you to loosen the grip that these thoughts have on you and make small incremental steps toward more productive thoughts, therefore building new branches between the neurons in the brain. These small steps are paramount when it comes to rewiring your brain and re-creating a reality that is fulfilling and satisfying. Finally, the nutrition and movement techniques help you build the health, strength, and motivation that you need to make all this happen. If you really want to go faster, face your fears!

Behaviors, Behaviors, Behaviors

Create your Wellness Mindmap, and select one area to work on. As described above, the Mindmap is intended to help you examine the key areas in your life where you can improve your health and your overall well-being. Decide which aspect of which area you would like to tackle first. Then get to work. Overcome excuses and hurdles to make it happen. This is your health we are talking about. As I suggested with your Stress Management Mindmap, take fifteen minutes first to create a draft of the Wellness Mindmap. Then block fifteen to thirty minutes on your calendar to continue working on it within the next few days and putting it into action.

Chapter 12: Graduation—The Road to Accomplishment and Happiness

Congratulations!

It is time to stop and acknowledge what you have accomplished in this leadership journey. Being able to acknowledge your accomplishments and others' accomplishments, small or big, is a leadership behavior in and of itself.

If you are having these nagging thoughts telling you that you could have accomplished more or that you didn't do well enough, this is an opportunity for you to transform these thoughts and focus on recognizing and fully appreciating what you have done! The road to accomplishment and happiness starts here. Otherwise, success remains elusive as you continue to chase the next thing, robbing yourself and your team of the joy, benefits, and lessons learned from the current endeavors.

Leadership in Review

Let's review the key takeaways of our leadership journey. This is what I want to leave you with:

1. Stopping

In a world of information overload and constant interruptions, we need to learn to stop! Not just randomly and aimlessly stop, but stop with specific intentions, namely three clear objectives:

- First, stop and focus.

- Second, stop and collaborate.

- Third, stop and play.

This is what I described as working in bursts. Unless we reinvent our workflow and start working in bursts and paying close attention to where we are in these cycles, as well as where our team is, leadership is a challenge. It is difficult to lead when we are overwhelmed and bouncing around from one interruption to the next at the mercy of the interrupters.

2. Thinking

Thinking involves reflecting and strategizing to become aware of what is not visible. This means getting underneath the surface and gaining depth. This also implies going way up above the surface and gaining perspective. Thinking also includes planning at all levels, from the micro-planning of the next twenty-minute task to the two week planning of our priorities to the longer term planning of the end results we are seeking. Thinking is the building block of self-awareness and awareness of others.

Leadership thinking involves but is not limited to:

- Thinking about our strengths and the strengths of others.

- Thinking about our style and the impact it has on others.

- Thinking about our thoughts and transforming them.

- Thinking and planning for our immediate priorities and end results.

- Thinking strategically and identifying our Deltas and Weak Links.

- Thinking with collaboration and teamwork in mind.

- Thinking creatively and innovatively.

3. Breaking things down

In a world of complexity, breaking things down into small components is vital:

- Breaking priorities and results down into actionable items with the Immediate Priorities Matrix and End Results Matrix.

- Breaking the current tasks down with Micro Planning.

- Breaking worries down with the Awareness Wheel.

- Breaking problems down with the Problem Solving Matrix.

- Breaking negotiations down with the Negotiation Matrix.

4. Feeling good

Accomplishments are only part of the journey. Another equally important part is feeling good and contributing to our team and organization feeling the same way. This means:

- Stopping often to get energizing breaks. Not letting thirty to forty-five minutes go by without stopping, even for a couple of minutes, for stretching or breathing.

- Managing stress with the Awareness Wheel.

- Identifying how our irrational thoughts are contributing to our stress and transforming them.

- Eating well to prevent disease, increase energy, and increase mental focus.

- Moving more to improve health, develop stamina, and get in a better mood.

- Encouraging and supporting others in their effort of feeling good.

5. Taking Action

It is all wishful thinking until we take action. Not just any action, but action on Deltas and action that is situational. Actions engage our senses, our thoughts, and our emotions, and therefore create our aha moments. This enables us to rewire our brain, instill lasting changes, and reach greater outcomes.

What is unique about a leader's actions is that they are the result of stopping, thinking, and breaking things down into smaller components. Such actions are substantially different from the ad-hoc actions and reactions that may otherwise unfold.

Additionally, in an era of information overload and too much to do with not enough time to do it, speed is essential when it comes to implementing our actions. The five elements of speed that I identified are:

1. Physical speed: Moving faster from point A to point B in whichever context we are in.

2. Mental speed: Staying focused during our Accomplishment Zone to accomplish amazing results in the shortest amount of time.

3. Strategic speed: Staying focused on the Deltas and keeping the Weak Links well under control.

4. Emotional speed: Getting over our thoughts and feelings quickly, and moving into our wants and actions

5. Psychological speed: Facing the fears, identifying our underlying distorted thoughts, and transforming them to free ourselves from their burden and move at warp speed in our leadership journey.

Now What!

The end is just the beginning of what is next. Now that this component of the leadership journey has ended, what is next for you in your leadership journey? Here are some ideas:

1. Create your own six-week follow-up plan

- Plan weekly reading and reflections.

- Revisit the key concepts and tools that we covered and apply them.

- Get more deeply into the topics that are most relevant to you.

- Set goals for this six-week journey that are similar to or a continuation of the goals discussed in chapter 1.

- Enlist someone to join you in this effort or be your accountability partner.

2. Continue learning

Plan the next learning adventure. As the growth mindset tells us, learning is an important part of growing and staying engaged. Learning can be formal or informal and can happen individually, in small groups, or in large groups. Be an opportunistic learner. Learn from everyone and every situation. Turn judgments into learning opportunities.

3. Get your team and organization on board

Coach them, mentor them, and encourage them to learn. After all, leadership is about inspiring people and creating results with people. It is much easier to lead when your followers are on the same page and have a common language, common best practices, and are aligned not only on goals and strategies but also on communication, problem solving, negotiation, and the various areas I discussed throughout the book.

4. Have a coach or a mentor

Implementation is where the rubber meets the road. A coach or a mentor can help make implementation smooth and successful. Even if you are a self-learner, getting input from objective and knowledgeable sources is likely to bring new perspectives and help you avoid blind spots. This effort can be formal or informal, and the more the coach or mentor already models the behaviors that you are trying to instill, the more likely they are suitable for you.

5. Be happy in the moment

On one hand, taking on a leadership journey is partly motivated by dissatisfaction with the status quo and the desire for things to be different from what they are today. On the other hand, this journey is partly about becoming satisfied in the present moment and not judging it but, rather, accepting it, reflecting on it, and planning the now what! This is quite a paradox. Are we dissatisfied or are we accepting? Can we be both? Or do we deploy the Working in Bursts model and alternate between intense moments of dissatisfaction that lead to creativity and innovation and moments of satisfaction that lead to appreciation and happiness? In whatever way you achieve it, embracing this paradox is the to road accomplishment and happiness.

Works Cited

Dweck, Carol. *Mindset: The New Psychology of Success.* New York: Random House, 2006.

Gordon, Evian. *Integrative Neuroscience: Bringing together biological, psychological and clinical models of the human brain.* Singapore: Harwood Academic Publishers, 2000.

Heath, Chip, and Dan Heath. *Switch: How to Change Things When Change Is Hard.* New York: Broadway Books, 2010.

Rath, Tom. *StrengthsFinder 2.0.* New York: Gallup Press, 2007.

Rath, Tom, and Barry Conchie. *Strengths Based Leadership: Great Leaders, Teams, and Why People Follow.* New York: Gallup Press, 2008.

Rock, David. "SCARF: a brain-based model for collaborating with and influencing others." *NeuroLeadership Journal*, 2008.

Zenger, John, and Joseph Folkman. *The Extraordinary Leader: Turning Good Managers Into Great Leaders.* McGraw-Hill, 2009.

Made in the USA
San Bernardino, CA
13 September 2014

Prison

ourneys

This Brighter Prison
A Book of Journeys

Karen Connelly

Brick Books

CANADIAN CATALOGUING IN PUBLICATION DATA

Connelly, Karen, 1969 –
  This brighter prison: a book of journeys

Poems.
ISBN 0-919626-63-7

I. Title.

PS8555.O55T5 1993   C811'.54   C93-093755-4
PR9199.3.C65T5 1993

Copyright © Karen Connelly, 1993.

The support of the Canada Council and the Ontario Arts Council
is gratefully acknowledged. The support of the Government of
Ontario through the Ministry of Culture and Communications is
also gratefully acknowledged.

Cover painting by Joane Cardinal-Schubert, 'The Banff Series-
Moonlight Sonata: Vision Quest', acrylic on canvas, 1989.
Photographed by John Dean.

Typeset in Ehrhardt, printed and bound by The Porcupine's
Quill. The stock is acid-free Zephyr Antique laid.

Second printing, September 1993.

Brick Books
Box 38, Station B
London, Ontario
N6A 4V3

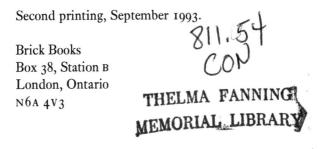

Acknowledgements

I gratefully acknowledge the former Alberta Foundation for Literary Arts and Alberta Culture, whose financial assistance enabled me to complete this collection.

I would like to thank the faculty and participants from the 1991 Banff May Studios, especially the late Adele Wiseman, who gave us so much grace. Thanks is also due, as always, to Nancy Holmes, and to Dennis Lee and Don McKay, my editor.

Some of these poems have appeared in their current or slightly altered forms in the following periodicals and anthologies:

Books In Canada, Dandelion, Descant, Grain, Guerra Azul (Spain), *More Garden Varieties II, Midwest Quarterly* (U.S.), *New Myths* (U.S.), *The New Quarterly, Passages, Poetry Canada, Prism International, Secrets from the Orange Couch, Stand* (England).

'Amaya' and 'Amaya, in spring' were aired on CBC's Alberta Anthology.

For my brothers and sisters,
Ken, Mara, David, Jen
and for Scott Gabriel.

Contents

Part I: Spanish Lessons

Part II: Paris Is Not A Dream

Part III: I Kneel To Kiss The Ice

Part IV: A Grand Place, A Greeting

The thing is to stalk your calling in a certain skilled and supple way, to locate the most tender and live spot and plug into that pulse. This is yielding, not fighting . . .

I think it would be well, and proper, and obedient, and pure, to grasp your one necessity and not let it go, to dangle from it limp wherever it takes you. Then even death, where you're going no matter how you live, cannot you part.

– Annie Dillard

Part I:　　❂　　Spanish Lessons

For Anayensi Lopez Herraiz

Spanish Lessons

Spain takes you in like a masked lover,
    ties you up with a red scarf,
    throws you the ocean's score
    and commands you to sing.
You are fooled by the grace of a man's hand
    gliding over a woman's bronze neck.
You are fooled by black eyelashes, amber eyes,
    mouths that smell of chocolate and wine.
Spain teaches that the body is its own absolute.
The body is greedy and simple, honest, a hungry child.
The Mediterranean insists that the mind
    is a snake in the sand,
    turning its sharp tongue in venom.

In El Greco's city of narrow streets, the sabres
    pierce your eyes to sunsets
    that awe even the gods.
Through a butterfly dance of bats, the violet sky
    sweeps down to kiss the velvet desert,
    reaches down to kiss your face,
    and stars drop ivory petals of light in your eyes.

The Old Man Presents Himself

Suddenly it is cold.
Green strokes of summer, a dream.
Burnt gold of fall, a good lie.
The sea beats its heart on the shore
     as fishermen beat tough octopi.
Water writhes into my life.
I must lie still, still, without slipping down.

Morning, but too cold to rise.
Tea from the tin–could it scald me to life?
The kitchen is a great distance from my bed.
The ceiling drips fine mud over my head.
Black pools poise to swallow my naked feet.

Now the Old Man presents himself at the roof
     and begins to eat.
I hear his mouth tear the tiles.
I hear his teeth break on the bricks.
He is crag-boned and blind.
His bitter sleep is a journey to fury.
His waking is a new storm.

Old Man Rain, old warlock:
I am wrapped up in wool.
I hide, whorled, almost impossible to pull from my shell.
I camp under my eyelids in less treacherous seasons.
Your mouth cannot touch me.

It takes one hundred years to erode
    a bowlful of stones,
    but in a winterkill of wind and rain,
    the mind's speckled shell cracks in a day.
I hear you lick at old faces bowed in doorways,
    at stray cats under stairs, at soft scars.
You seep into my crooked joints.
That is where you try to enter me, Old Man,
    through the once-broken bones in my hand.
I clench my fingers to force you out
    but will you ever really leave me?
I wait, I lie quietly.

You knock knuckles high on my chest.
No answer there.
This body is a hollow husk.

You fill it with your cold silver,
    your winking rain-coins
    and coiled whips of wind.
You seep through the shutters.

I may drown this way, a little rain
    in my nose, in my eyes.
Even now I do not rise.
It is late morning and I do not rise.

Ana Falls In Love With A Rich Man

I From her notebook:

Love is a mess on sheets that should have been washed last week.
I hate this country, this stone town. Tragic glory sickens me.
Love is small and oval, peculiar on the tongue, a blue fruit,
clearly poisonous. Yet how willingly I gulp it down. Love is
sobbing idiotically on park benches, in cafés, over sinks, on
toilets, on balconies. On balconies, of course! What's a woman
without a balcony and tears? Love is my long black hair ruined,
wet with sperm and my own saliva. Love is dirty hair: I have not
showered for a week. The faucet has rotted out of the wall.

Remember the nun's prayer: Glory, etc., for heaven, may God
soon lift life's filthy burden from us forever. Amen.

II During the day, Ana rubs silverware.
Her face is dry.
Her green-veined arms are bare.
The gilt dishes insinuate queens
into her dull afternoons.
She wears a black skirt
to dress another woman's child.

At dusk, she searches for her name,
finds her umbrella, walks voiceless
and beautiful through the raining streets.
She sees ballet dancers with willow arms
pirouetting on the roofs.
Her hands are raw.
For supper she drinks coffee,
dips her biscuits like a raccoon,
all dark eyes, quick paw.

In the evening she runs
shadow to shadow,
slips quickly through the alleys,
whispers his name to her callouses.
She greets the strays, hops over used needles
and whispers, Oh sweet addiction.
She waits at his gate
and cries when he doesn't come.

Then Ana hurries home,
face wet, muscles grown stiff.
She leaves her heart in the doorway,
curled up and beating beside the cat
who gnaws a dead mouse.

She leaves her earrings
on the doormat of his house,
she leaves red carnations
and clicks away over the moon-wet cobblestones.
Even at night, the light sears.
Ana hides from the ruthless shine of cars.

She does not look at the stars:
they might crash down on her,
they are too sharp.

Her hair is a torn scarf.
Her face is Japanese-white,
a rare blossom that opens
only at night.
Her eyes are ebony seeds
floating in salt water.

Amaya

'Do you know what it is to be touched
by a human being?' – Anaïs Nin

Out of the mouth of darkness
     the rain's glass teeth
     shatter on the tiles.
There is no one here but myself

(the train station past midnight:
 belly of gnawed cigarette butts,
 shuddering newspapers,
 lustrous signatures of spittle)

And a small animal curled under a bench
(a million feet have touched here
 and a million feet have blinked
 away from what they've seen)

When will the train come?
From its ragged snare of bones, I know
     she's wounded, easier to kill than to save.
She begins to shake.
With my warm eyes, I prod her awake.
She crawls out in a flood of hair.
A cat? A crippled dog?
She whines words I do not know
     navaja navaja
Her eyes are human enough
     but my vocabulary is deficient.
I am only waiting for the train to come.

When the last of the line arrives
     my hands are numb.
The stray chatters, chews at her wrist-bone.
Like a night-scatter of clothes,
          (soiled shirt, stinking slips of cloth,
                    necessary filth)

I lift her tattered bag of skin.
Inside the train, her body falls fluid,
    pliant as a fresh-shot rabbit,
    she slides off the seat,
    curls up, head hooded with hands,
        far and safe from my feet.
A mangy flock of men gaze at us,
        each one drunk, each one
        a hard-mouthed goat.

Navaja? Perhaps it is her name.

    *   *   *   *   *

In my house, there is one narrow bed.
Like a dog, she sleeps on the floor beside it.
I am too young to be her mother,
    but she is a daughter
    who has bad dreams.
When her body dries, it is a breathing crow's nest.
Her eyes glisten like two of those hungry birds.

For the first week, she will only say
    My name is Amaya
    I am too thin.
But Amaya cannot eat.
She sucks at a glass of thick juice,
    fears the hard red apples,
    the great hearts of vegetables.
You eat those? she whispers, cringing.
Yes, Amaya. Those are carrots.

At night I lie awake as Amaya wrestles
    the starving blue snakes in her body.
She narrates her battles to the darkness.
I keep a dictionary beside me and loose my fingers
    after her strange words.

Navaja, from the train station, is a switchblade.
Jeringuilla is a syringe.
Bicho is a small animal, snake, or maggot.
Amaya is my teacher of graceless phrases.

Once, leaning on an elbow, looking down
   at her blanched and crooked face, I heard a ghost.
I've never seen one, but I felt one's voice
   shiver up to my shoulders:
   it was the shadow of a child in song.
That night, Amaya grew a pink flower of a tongue
   and tossed its petals in the air.

Her flesh tongue is moth-eaten,
   nicked by a needle, a scrap
   of red silk pricked with holes too rotten
   to soak up the soft cotton insides of bread.

Like all miracles, Amaya must be witnessed
   or she would not exist.
She subsists solely on water and egg-whites,
   drawing a skim of strength
   that will freeze and shatter
   in winter's gaunt jaws.

The ice here does not harden outside.
It grows wetly in houses, on floors, between sheets.
Winter in any land is a season of failing.
Only this rain remains faithful.
Only the clouds have great integrity.
They drain themselves to stillness.
I hoard my thick blood, though,
   and urge the girl to go.

Sometimes she does not wake.
I step over her head in the morning.
She can sleep whole days while her heart
    plaits and unplaits its own death.
I wait for her to steal from me, or drown her veins
    in one last rush, the ecstatic flush down the needle.
But Amaya doesn't die here.

The day before she disappears
    she cleans the house with a brittle sorrow,
    the way you clean the cupboard of someone
        who has loved you
          but died.

She scratches her knees, bangs her shins.
She cracks the mirror, leaves drawers open,
    knots undone, the bucket unemptied.
That is why I will never kill myself,
        she laughs.
    I can never finish the work.
    Look, she says, look at these,
        cicatrices.
Beneath bracelets and leather, the scrawl
    of two red scars.

The next morning, Amaya is not beside me.
I find a trail of feathers and bits of fur.
The dirty water sours in its bucket.
She scurries into the spider-streets,
coughs and greets the granite ribs of winter.

I did not stop her.
I did not say goodbye.
I was asleep.

Very quickly the dirty water begins to rot.
It might never have been clean.
During a storm, I pour it from a window,
      watch it search out a gutter
      like a gray-shedding snake.
The cracked mirror remains though.
I grow accustomed to seeing my cleft face.

Amaya, in spring

Amaya has come home
though that word is not quite right.
She has returned with chips of winter
    stuck in her teeth

    but it is spring now.

The air is smooth as the flesh over a man's ribs.
Just touching grass, just treading quietly
    is almost as easy and far gentler
        than making love.
The wind breathes Africa on us and the sea
    is a sweet juice squeezed up over the sand.
Azkorri's children go to the cliffs
    and lean backwards into the wind,
    praying to rise like kites.
In the tradition of the new season
        Amaya
(my drug addict, my breaker of mirrors)
        is pregnant.

A memory of my mother laps on one of my messier shores.
She is drowning quietly in the slough
    of my dead sister's clothes
    clutching a flimsy rope of gold,
    coughing, 'But she was so beautiful,'

    as if that was enough
    as if that was anything at all.

Yet that is what I think myself
    when I hear Amaya in my bathroom,
    shaken like a rug by her furious belly,
    rippling again and again over the toilet.

I whisper to the wall: God, she is so beautiful,
    knowing this is neither an excuse
    nor a prayer.

For a month, she scratches around for a willing doctor
in this Catholic maze of whitewashed houses,
this village whipped to chastity by winter sleet.
The only abortionist is the greedy surgeon
(forensic) who wastes Sundays
drinking with her stepfather (policeman).
He calls her a whore.
A trip to France is the only door
out of her iron-maiden body.

The year does not matter, nor the country,
nor this spiced green season.
Beauty is a talisman in myths she never learned.
It does not guide her now,
alone on the other side of the border,
slipping against oiled French words.
She dreams awake of serrated edges and steel knives.
This is anywoman's dream, in every country, every season,
but the irony of spring amuses Amaya.

She comes back with a white grin, lips tight as scars.
A fever of infection reddens in her
but she is blessedly hollow
as a cathedral's carved dome.
She makes a bed on my floor and sleeps for two days.

Amaya's body remains what it was
when I first found her, slightly thicker
than her skeleton, a famine's dog.
She picks at boiled potatoes, sucks at milk and eggs,
grimacing, exhausted by nourishment.

She almost stayed pure this winter,
heaved heroin again
and again out of her ransacked veins.
But her tongue (a tidy hiding-place for needle-marks)
is still a painter's rag for red oils.

When I watch Amaya's face, I hear another woman rasping
    at my back, her face draped in deeper shadow.
Once she said, It is easier to be a memory
            than it is to be alive.

Amaya, she lied.
See yourself,
    the pitch river of hair
    spilling down the ravine of your back,
    bones pearled in pale velvet, raven-eyes.
Amaya, I whisper, go gently.
A talent for sorrow is almost
    a talent for love.
Only the key is different.
Sing until you find the other sound.

I speak to the night while she sleeps by my bed.
She rolls over.
A white hand hooks like a cloud
    between the steep ridge of hips and ribs.
Amaya lies dreaming on the floor,
    her bones warping in rancid blood.

Would You Trade Your Life To Live There?

The days at Sopelana unroll like bolts
     of cinnamon cloth, warm weaves
     of red wine and perfumed skin.
The sun paints her people with amber oil.
Roses grasp the iron gates.

We walk slowly down to the water,
     down the steps of turquoise moss.
Lizards dance into the secret mouths of stone.
The sea below us pulses its sun-alive heart
     towards our bodies, a marine wolf
        pierced green by light.

You ask if I would trade my life. . .
     trade the acid pleasure of this air
     for gleaming scales.

Yes. Yes.
Let's not pretend.
We both know what lurks
behind this arras of roses and sun.

Why don't you believe me?
I would like to shed the weight
     of human skin,
     pare away these blunt bones.
I could quit it, spit it down
     among the salt-eaten ears of shells,
        this life,
     and leave it for the water.

Give me the pearl brain of a fish
  flying weightless through blue glass

  alive for moments only
    but perfect,
      perfect
  plying the shining blood
    of a god
    who never lies.

Rat Laughter

At night, memory comes to play its game
    in the shadows of Maria Cristina—
        el parque de los viejos.
It is the place I go to watch the sea,
    the lost lovers, the hungry rats—
        the park of the old ones.

The laughter of the rats is sharp, so sharp
    I cut my ears listening to it.
Later I wander home with crimson ribbons wet on my neck.
Rat laughter gnaws the fleshy braid twisted on the bench.
Rat laughter nibbles those fragrant ropes,
        that forearm, that flank,
        her long hair as it caresses the dust.
But the lovers do not feel the small yellow teeth
        slash open their shadows
        when the rats march through the dew.

The lovers feel nothing but each other.
They are wrapped in a blanket of velvet,
        shoulders brushed with starlight.
Their bodies melt together like brown sugar.
The rats smell this sweetness.
They shriek with glee.
But still the lovers do not hear, cannot see.

Then the rats turn, spit their vision
        through darkness and chuckle at me.
The professor's specimens never giggled like this.
And these rats do not wear silk coats of white.
Their fur is scavenged by night, welted with mud.
Their eyes are not a shade of weak blood.
Their eyes are small black mouths that do not close
        when I am sleeping.

These rats are untouchable.
They cannot be caged or counted.
The belly of Europe twitches with them.

II The smell of the lovers with their brown-sugar skin,
        the rats in the darkness with their fur tinted blue,
        these midnight details make me lonely for you.
    Memory comes to play its game in Maria Cristina.
    I recall chalk-dust mapping your hands,
        your wet-fur smell of formaldehyde.

    I remember searching for mysterious shrews with you,
        scrambling over mountains to bang on hollow trees.
    We leaned earthward on hands and knees
        to peer into the oracle of rodents.

    Once you were my teacher,
    brought me hundreds of books,
    taught me how to read—
    then I left you.

    Does my memory still make ashes flower in your mouth?
    Do you still wake with thorns wedged between your teeth?

    These Latin rats remind me of you,
        the hours you spent among cages and wriggling souls.
    I look out over the sea and know
        how your laboratory hums and squeaks,
        how your back aches in the yellow light.

    All this wet salt and distance,
        and still we are not strangers.
    Even if the body is different, flesh is flesh,
        the air is rough in every country.
    I soothe my rawness with an ocean.
    You experiment with new hearts.
    We cleave away from what we love
        to shed the burned skin.
    The lovers in the park, when they part, learn this.

    And the laughing rats rush in.

Teeth Of Garlic

But I do not think of guilt,
    says the young woman.
We are speaking Spanish.
I have learned the rolling sounds and now
    an ocean raves in my ear.
A birth, entrance to this language, I greet keen air.
There is a sensation akin to pain,
    and light savage to the eye,
        then the shock that comprehension does not matter.
She would talk to the water-heater if I weren't here.

I don't remember guilt.
We perch like starlings in the kitchen,
    a cascade of brick-coloured light
    falling on our hands and faces.
In the streets below, roller-skates rattle
    over cobblestones, a puppy yelps, summer
    winds up through the window like hot emerald ivy.
An Arab with a voice like a satin broom
    is selling carpets in another street,
    sweeping in the sweet glow of dusk.
If he were white and singing, women would want him.

She smokes a cigarette delicately,
    a heron drinking water.
She leans her head back to inhale,
    eyes green in this light,
    gray in shadow,
    teeth always invisible,
        the black ones at the front hidden
            behind the lips,
        the lips hide the tongue,
            the tongue knows everything,
            the tongue is the snake whose every scale
                is a memory, a face and its name
                and a gutted cry.

I just remember his hands, she confides
 to the water-stained walls.
They smelled like garlic.
He smelled like garlic.
Ajo in Spanish, the j is guttural,
 it's a different sound altogether,
  from the throat.
Not a clove, *un diente.*
There were teeth of garlic cut open
 on the cutting table, ropes of garlic
  hanging from the ceiling.

She pulls a chair close to her,
 lifts up her bare feet, toes like cracked sculpture,
  lines of dirt, a blister.
A long scar twitches up her ankle.
Why are you staring at my feet? she asks,
 and our sudden clash of laughter
 disturbs the blue nooses of cigarette smoke.
I do not tell her that I am hunting
 for details, rooting around
 like a barn animal after scraps.
That I believe bits of bone and gristle are magic.
That I believe the silt of hearts is flecked with gold.

The girl spills memory into me
 and I open like an eager hand
  to catch her words,
  the history of the cook in her mother's bar,
  fingers and teeth of garlic,
   her own late nights washing dishes,
   serving the policemen's tables,
  La Guardia Civil with their brown backs,
   black eyes, smooth as Dobermans,
  their hard little hands implying power,
   Just the way they drink from wine glasses

used to make me cringe, she says,
I always thought they would break glass
by holding it.
I wasn't strong then, I was still so tiny
(she makes a small diameter of her hands)
my waist like this, and long hair,
and my face—
(and shakes her head and laughs like a crow)
I looked like a duckling, so soft, so bright
(she pushes the chair away, pads over to the balcony,
leans far out)
I was a little fool. Why does no one
tell us anything when we are that small?
I was twelve.

I hid my first two months
of bloodied panties in a shoebox
until my mother found them
and tossed them, wounded rose doves,
all over the house, in front of my brothers.
She even flung a few out the windows, screeching
about convents and filth.
I was a little fool, like all little girls.

And the man with the teeth of garlic
was called Aitor, Basque,
dark blond, big as a Percheron.
I will never forget him.
I hated him once but now
it's all right,
I thank anyone who drags me
into the light,
into the storm.
Life is a storm, you know.

She glances over her shoulder, winks
    above that disk of bone brown as coffee,
        and smiles now, stretches her young lips
            into a hag's mouth, black ivory rotting her jaw.
Storm in Spanish is *tormenta*.
La vida es una tormenta, she says.
She knows gentleness is a savage trick.

It was better in the kitchen when I was twelve
and the men were watching soccer in the bar,
cheering, shouting, my mother. . .
—I don't know where she was—
Idurre was cutting the tortilla de patata.
My brother was pouring out Patxaran.
It seemed to be a party, someone's party.
La vida es una tormenta.
I don't remember exactly,
just the garlic, God, God,
the reek of garlic on me,
        inside of me

I didn't understand, I thought
    it had to be done in the dark, I never
    imagined a kitchen, the knives there, the peppers
    hanging like the wrinkled faces of elves, the hams
        strung up and ugly above me.

Aitor lifted me like a small trophy
    and nailed me to the wall.
My spine was a snake torn open.
A corkscrew opened me, I am sure
I screamed but the soccer, I could hear
    cheering, television, my brother
    whistling while wiping counters.
It takes longer to tell than it took to happen.
Aitor was heaving like a horse after a hunt,
    napkins in his hands for me,
        blood down my legs.

Oh, my sweet barbarians.
If you write this, write it in Spanish, no,
in Basque, Euskara, my country's oldest language.
I want to nail it to the door of San Ignacio,
to the door of my mother's house,
to the door of the bar,
every bar,
to the petrified wood of the skulls here.
España, tierra del matador.
When I saw my own blood,
I thought men were bulls,
made to gore.

The Ugly Mermaid

Late nights alone by water,
salted wind tears my face
like a rough-tongued cat.
The air is a black bruise,
the old lighthouse a hard lover.
Light pours from his mouth but never touches mine.
The glowing warm tongue is swallowed.

I walk away, I run, knead my feet in the dirty sand.
There are smooth chiselled bones here, bleak amethysts
of glass, fish shredded to satin tassels.
I dance over the bloated belly of a cat from the wharf.

I dream of dear Jonah and whales, but tragic miracles are rare.
I come away with kelp and jellied ghosts embroiled in my hair.
I cleave my knees on grinning rocks, rip bits of shirt and chest.
But my deepest wounds are salt stains on new leather shoes.
Later, a mad fish, I quit the sea.

My eyes are silver disks.
My fingers are stiff webs, but the water doesn't want me.
At home, I dance in my own blue arms.
I hum in a red net of hair.

My mirror sings a song:

> sea-witch, ugliest mermaid,
> a siren who seduces only herself,
> you are cast out, clenched of heart,
> you make a ragged voyage in the dark
>
> and even the sea spits you out
> like a rotten tooth.

A Song For Lorca
or, A Lament For The Madness Of Spanish Fiesta

Fool, you're lost again.
Searching for a country that doesn't exist.
You passed the small islands painted in mist
and disembarked on the wrong shore.
All night, on this muddy beach, caged lions
pace and growl, pace and roar.
They dream of a scarlet savannah
and a fat gazelle.

You find a carnival run by drunken clowns.
Their brass-horn voices burst in your ears.
People pour around you, streams
of enormous spawning fish, skins slick
and glittering.
They never say it but death
breathes on the tip of their tongues.
Only drinkisshriek
breaks from their mouths.
They don't see their costumes splitting,
sequins spitting up like lost teeth.
Men whirl women by the waist,
toss green-streamer screams in the air.

Every noise has colour:
The marching band plays jolting red.
The guns and bells burn off blue shocks.
Child-squeals are piercing yellow fading brown.

Can you hear them singing up in the town?
Songs like whipped horses rear from their mouths,
charge and gallop over cliffs
into the sea's silver maw.
Can you hear?

The people leap like insects
to beaten music, throats dry
as grasshoppers' thighs.
The men buzz like warm flies.

A reeking garden of wine-roses
and smoke and putrid beer
blossoms over night.
A farm is here, horses, preening birds
black and crimson, a small slaughter
house of bulls with frothing backs.
A strong beast staggers before the crowd,
tripping on ropes of his own blood.
Men rake the sand and begin to cheer again.

The gypsies drift in from nowhere,
the only country they love.
Their eyes do not spill gold light.
Even the children's skin is worn tight.
Squeezing rags from his accordion,
a father watches his dirt-bronzed daughter
prance over sunflower shells.
The man doesn't grind out *alegria* but sells
sad jingles and fistfuls of garlic.
His clan comes with their long-horned goat
and a wagonload of ducklings.

The ducklings are dyed blue, green,
bright peach, a hundred pesetas each,
waddling bodies of candy-floss,
melt-in-the-mouth animals.

Crowds coil around to buy them, arms stretch out,
quick-muscled children slink around legs.
In *fiesta*, the people will buy ducklings,
everyone wants to play.
The ochre-lipped gypsies nod and smile.
They know every soft creature dies in a day.

Isadora and the Basque Photographer

Quickly, Iñaki, take her picture
    catch the light and her hand
        spread on the whitewashed wall,
        hold the lizard there, above her skull
        warming leather in the sun,
        its eyes slit to feathers of gold.

Quickly, the photograph,
    trap this moment, the shadows
    playing like purple flowers on her face
    as she throws her head back to laugh.

The girl is laughing,
    her mouth is cleft fruit, wet,
    her golden hand splays against white,
    the bones are perfect, flowing from fingers
        to wrists to elbows to neck
        like the glimmering cables
        of a sun-struck bridge.

My body is a bridge, she tells you, smiling.
There is always someone crossing over.

Iñaki, quickly, take the picture,
    remember her this way,
        Sunday afternoon on Skopelos,
        grief sleeping in a sea
        the same colour as your eyes.

You have missed a thousand other moments of her life.
You were too breathless to take pictures
    when she was naked on the beach,
    singing for no reason.
You inhaled her voice and nearly choked,
            but she chuckled as watermelon seeds
                fell on her belly,
                oh, the pink juice, she said,
                    and pulled your head down
                        to lick her clean.

Even as she swam, you only stared
    at the gloves of blue water stroking her body.
You cannot photograph any of that,
    or the years she has picked grapes
    and found fine Greek men to fuck.

She leans against the wall of the white church.
All the walls leading up and away are white,
    or blue, azure, draped with sleeping cats and flowers,
    fuschia and flame cascading over every fence.

Her body will be the arched bridge beneath you,
    you will cross over her,
    pound over her, running,
        rushing, the flesh on her skeleton
            will be pale as a clay road
                under the moon.

The church is two hundred years old.
Her face will not last that long.
You will die.
Take the photograph.
You are dying now.

The colours will never be like this again.
Blind old men will wander home from the docks,
    dazed by the stench of dead fish and feline sex.
As the water roils to darkness, the sky will raise
    the rotting face of a black angel.

In late evening, Isadora's smooth-plank back
    will snap away from your bed.
She will fling open every door and window in this house,
    weary of your rich skin,
        sickened by the brackish musk of your love.

A Painting For Rachel

Rachel is dead.
Like a woman rolling over in bed,
I greet the emptiness beside me.

At the funeral, they forgot what I look like.
No one's eyes hold me still
and I do not feel God's eyes either.

(Rachel always said, God's eyes are on you.)

If he ever had eyes, he has taken them out now.
He sleeps poorly.
I dream he is old English and drinks weak tea.
He pulls his blanket over a bony knee.
I could love a sad god
who never really meant it,
who was mistaken and tangled
in the string of constellations.
If he had tripped on Andromeda,
burnt his ankle and fallen chin-first
in this muck of earth, I might call him Father.

Something was wrong with me as a child.
Even in daylight I lived strange dreams, made
        subtle connections
                between the whispering pages of the Bible
                and lengths of lilac toilet paper.
But how she loved His book, His rock dungeons
        and polished wood, the worn grooves of grieving hands.
Everything stinks of candles and rotting skin.
She is dead.

Will I forget her as easily
      as I forget the animals
      and men I have deeply loved?
What I remember is imagined, this poem
      is imagined, this is a history
      I give myself, a rug of scraps
      well-woven, yanked over the holes.
Can we ever know well what we love
      when all the traces of flesh
      on flesh are so frail?
Even bruises disappear.
The wind licks away our echoes.
The days do not turn slowly now.

I paint a goblin running riotous
through the woods, cackling,
head tossed back,
serpent-hair seething ticks.
This is a picture of time.
A god is also in the painting, many gods,
      stretching their tempered bones
      into the sky's heart.
Time races down among their shadows.
Rachel never knew these gods.
The ones I love.

They rise above our cathedrals of despair.
Their fingers traverse, twine tender light,
      sign a language Rachel never learned.
Gods of the true tongue,
      they have no word for 'sin'

            no words at all,
                  yet they sing for us, sing,

                        demanding and offering
                        the crucial gift of air.

A Bowl Of Yellow Flowers Stains The Canvas

Here is a broad stone wall flicking alive small green flames of lizards. The wall is low: I sit on its back, watching the road that curves around the wet blue belly of the sea. The sea is always itself, restless, forever altering its colours like a sad eye; the road itself never shifts; the squat wall I balance on is the tough arm of an old fisherman. It keeps children and old women from dancing off the cliffs.

Here we are, *los domingueros*, the Sunday people, drunk to exhaustion with light and the dusty scent of African wind. The bright blue benches behind me are soft with the bodies of old people, tense with the knuckles and knees of young lovers. The old people wait patiently for the farther darkness, the young for the closer one. They sigh anxiously, almost painfully, glancing in happy anguish at each other's fingers and chins.

If you sit on a bench, the wall cuts the landscape in half: you cannot see the road below or the little restaurant on the beach where black guard-dogs sit on the roof, glaring at customers. From a bench, the landscape is picturesque: you receive the sea rising up like a mirror to the sky, slow ships sweeping the harbour like women in evening gowns, the grand old mansions governing the far cliffs.

If you sit on the wall (but no one else does, for sun, olives, and wind unbalance, and the drop would be lethal), you get a wider angle. The back-arch of the waves stretches towards you, warm as a cat begging hands. There is something about the sea that makes you want to reach out.... Below, the beach is speckled with people, scurrying with energetic crabs and children and dogs. The dogs are bounding through sand, barking, pleading with stones to come alive and throw themselves into the air. The dogs see, blissfully, with their noses. They are enthusiastic about dead squid. From here, it looks clean: children tumbling playfully, doll-limbed, the people (featureless, really, at this distance) fine and strong, leaving well-formed footprints behind them. But you also recall occasional smudges of tar, the condom-scatter of spent Catholic boys on Saturday mornings, the shredded glitter of dead fish. Still, from the wall, the scene gleams, glassed-over, lovely.

But the view includes the road, which I watch in amazement. The thud bangs in my own bones as I realize what I've seen: a

child and a car have collided with the grace of birds; it was choreographed, her skipping down off the path and the black swoop of metal speeding around, catching her at the waist. Her scream is mistaken for a seagull's. There are thirty people behind me, oblivious as I watch a shadow dyeing the road (it does not even appear red–simply dark, like dirt spilling from a bowl of yellow flowers, her head).

There are shouts below, the single wail of a woman, but still no one around me hears this, no one leans over to look. I wonder if I am imagining all of it. I blink away sunlight and the cracked body remains down there, utterly still. The people around me (half-hearing the female cry) think only that the beat of the waves has changed.

The old people are gazing at the cliffs, ignoring the white threads of cataracts, seeing perfectly the greenness of other lives, other decades, thinking of the ancient lime trees towering beyond them–they were smaller once. I hear serious talk about green beans and rose gardens, the cost of carrots. The laughter of sparrows rings from the trees as always, and the young men and women listen to it, imagining their hearts are birds. A girl with hair the colour of clean straw is staring at her watch, desperate for time to slide open. Her hand flutters at the boy's silk-brown arm and I can see what her fingers are thinking: there has never been flesh this warm. Their hair is tangled and heavy with dropping light. The sun rolls down the hill like bleeding fruit.

And on the road below (all I do is swivel three vertebrae in my neck) the scene changes, a world bursts, the magic shadow spreads like a dark angel stretching its wings under people's feet. The bowl of yellow flowers is a rust-red brown.

While above, in the little town, old women gossip, girls touch lipstick lightly to their mouths, men grunt at the government, and I sit on the wall, watching all of it, looking back and forth like someone at a stunning tennis match, trembling (remembering all the newspapers I haven't read, remembering the world itself, the wars in the back pages of atlases, whole countries spreading with shadow).

This is where you are now. Then you turn your head away and you are somewhere else. The only truth is that there is none: it

moves when we blink. The trick of seeing is not seeing everything. If you see everything and feel all you see, you unravel the wrinkles of your brain like a ball of kite string. You drift off and disappear. It is easier to be blind if the choice is between blindness and madness. Learn to see with one eye or both eyes half-closed. I look at the lovers, the lavender-haired old ladies. I look with great concern at my bony feet. Absurd tears there, gems of wet salt sliding towards my toes.

Because, below, a child drains. The moment was a pebble-brained shark, and her life a tear in time's soft belly. Now an ambulance clangs everyone awake, the people, even the lovers, crowd to see the crowd below, to glimpse the broken doll, the shadow. A shattered body collapses in my eyes, but I look beyond it. I examine the elegant web of veins on the backs of my hands. (You must look beyond.) I see the Bay of Biscay. I slide off the wall and walk towards a new place. The blood on the road will be gone at dawn.

Here are the pastel hues (skylight, sea, warm green eyes, pearled skin). And here are the dark oils. And here is your life. This is the only canvas they'll sell you. Do not paint what there is. (You'll be dust before you've done that work.) Paint what you want to see.

Part II: ☼ Paris Is Not A Dream

Paris Is Not A Dream

I   Are there days?
    Or only streets and paintings?
    The catacombs of the city are mapped
        by calloused feet.
    The heels of businessmen
        peel from frenzied walking.
    Do not offer your hand.
    There will be a great rushing-in,
        a blur of feather, fur, fin.
    Animals of all sorts feed here.

    There are no leafy interiors,
        no weedy fields of crickets,
        no bouquets of hay and sky.
    The parks stink of snapdragons and sex.
    This is the Fine City, the Legend,
        any city, it seethes.
    People live here, and die.
    Their skin barely breathes.

    Paris is not a dream
    but a lie, a lace-at-the-throat duel,
    a swordfight in red,
    a shaken marionette
    exquisite
    and dead.

II The old staircase swirls like a shell
        up to the soft centre,
        the nest of raw silence that hides you.
    You perch above the filthy sea of streets,
        feet cold on clay-stained tiles.
    The bones in your toes crack when you rise.

The city bellows a famished roar.
You pick up the mouldy fists of bread from the floor,
    the little clumps of cheese,
    the broken wine glass:
        you hurl it all out to the gargoyles.
At night, you dream of trees
    but wake to a weed of sun in the sky.
Time pools quickly in the gutters under your eyes.

Each morning you journey underground,
    rake through the pocked and perfect faces.
You search for the mask whose fissures
    are wide enough for your fingers.
But the Metro is tight and dry.
Her people fear your wet eyes.

Your face is round and bright,
    an innocent marble.

III Men want to roll you back and forth
as you roll their names off your tongue.
Liqueurs and blue oysters slink down your throat.
So much hot bone draped with glinting skin
and fine cologne!
Jean-Louis, Jabar the Arab, Didier,
Dominique, Erik the mad Dane, etc.
Each cultured one an affectionate rapist.
Men stream and scatter like cockroaches.

Afterwards, you say to the neck
    of a man you cannot see:
    I'm going for a walk now.
You rise; he does not open his eyes.
You take your walk like you take your tea,
    too quickly, gulping distance,
        burning your mouth on the acrid blackness.

Night wraps you up in a wet veil,
 sticks in your nose,
  stretches its purple tail
   down your throat.

You sing under the bridges.
You watch rats eat old bread.
Half-drowned songs float in your head.
At night, the city is made of bricks, sewers,
  dregs of beautiful bodies,
  scraps of heart sinking in fountains.
Deep in St. Denis, bored prostitutes
 rinse their mouths of dirty rain.
Blue flesh bangs blue flesh, fiascos
 of neon creatures trapped by eyes.

Watching those bodies, you remember
 the men you've kissed,
 the tears pissed away in half-darkness
 beside foreign skin.
You clutch the little book in your fist,
 but your words are hiding.
The river pants like a dog on your face.
You remember your other country,
 but it is so far from this place.
The broken compass is wedged in your chest.
You neither run nor rest, but wait,
 your baffled eyes open wide.

IV In the museums and churches,
  hands like blades pass through your body,
  lives waltz into your skeleton,
  fingers press your eyelids

  and the whisper of history is such
  that you cannot hear your own blood.

Ghosts carry away pieces of your shadow in their mouths.
The lips of paintings brush your face.
There is blood in the oils, bones in the bronze,
    hearts churned into the walls,
    vast red bricks of memory.
The canvas is skin, the clay is meat.
Lives, stories, deaths, lives blaze silently around you,
    inhabiting your mind like a herd of fine-eyed horses.
You feel hooves pound against your cranium.

Christ is still pinned to our sin like a dragonfly.
In portraits that smell of spring, children
    are pressed shining among roses and dahlias.
You wander dazed through centuries,
    through fields of caught lives,
    mountains, deserts in Egypt—
        the gentle faces of camels
        turn to skulls before your eyes.

You plunge through midnight seascapes.
The moon's luminous hair sticks to your lips.
Night's black lace melts over your eyes
    at two in the afternoon.
Daggers from India are driven deep through your mind.
You trudge over frozen-fleshed snow,
    almost touch the frost-eaten fingers of soldiers.
The desolate light of these winters is so sharp
    your own eyelids stiffen with cold.

Pheasants and rabbits hang like brown tongues of silk.
Their bodies slip over the edges of tables,
    mouths crimson with detail.
Vegetables around them are just ripe enough to eat,
    orange and green, and fruit swollen with juice.
Just under the warm canvas, the yellow apples are cool.

You want to strip your body of clothes, your mouth
    of tinsel words, you want to drop your twisted yarn
        of brain on the floor
        and plunge into the paintings,
        greet the cracked and open faces,
        faces like roasted chestnuts,
        warm and raw, eaten centuries ago,
            but still here,

        lives, stories, deaths, lives,
        more vibrant in paint than
        your own sweating fingers,
        faces, eyes, touching yours.

You feel hands in your hair, you hear the drunken songs,
    the weeping violins, the prayers of dying nuns,
    music mixed oil three hundred years ago.

In the empty galleries, there is a dazzle of windows,
    webs of glass entangling light.
The sun pierces the speckled body of day
    with golden claws.

That is what you want, everything:
    the old dream
    of drawing gold
  from the quick dust
    of moments.

In Versailles, the gilded horses are still,
    still rising
    gold out of the filthy water.

Jean-Louis, eight years after the Italian girl went away

Jean-Louis,
we call you a clown,
a buffoon: the word matches your nose,
your foolish blue eyes.
We call you an idiot,
but how we love your fragile heart
of feathers and wine.
You lean over your paintings
groaning, tears in your eyes.
You wail at us sometimes,
when you are drunk,
pleading, pleading

and how we laugh at you!

Such melodrama!
Your sadness is too grand for us.
We have scrappy little hearts made of tin.
You could wash the blue houses bright red
        with the blood of your mourning dove's heart.
Your sadness coats every stone on this island.
Your longing is turquoise and big as the bay,
        precious as the fish there, glinting,
        transparent and dangerous as the medusas
                gloating in the depths.
You say that the men-of-war are so flimsy,
                so lovely, dark lavender, red,
                they remind you of her lingerie.

And you paint her again and again that way,
    in a nightdress made of shadow,
    her limbs and breasts blue in moonlight,
    her entire face open as a mouth,
    one hand stroking her naked neck.
The stars in this painting are too radiant.
She is standing on the terrace, looking
    at something alien to the canvas,
    the outskirts of Florence, perhaps,
    to some rich man's unromantic factory.
Jasmine yearns towards her, its white flowers
    the living lace of fragrance.
If we look long enough at the portrait,
        the gentle spice of jasmine rises,
            wafts out of the paint
                to exhaust our lungs.
            We breathe in and in, we want
                to crush those flowers in our fingers.

Even as we laugh at you, Jean-Louis,
and shake our heads,
we inhale your paintings
as if they were perfume
drifting vivid from the skin of Venus.
We have no sacred loves.
When we say she cannot be as
beautiful as you remember,
we know we are lying.

The Jeweller In Brazil

For R.F., who claimed that Paris was a city of angels.
'El universo me cuida muy bien.'

It is a strange history for an Anglo-Austrian diamond-cutter.
Twenty years ago, you did not know the price
    of silk shirts from Italy.
You did not love Paris; you had never been there.

You were wandering markets in the Andes, through Brazil,
    hair long as a woman's and the colour of light,
    eyes so bright that the coffee-skinned children
        watched you from doorways and skittered
        like rabbits if you came too close.

The evenings were longer there than anywhere
    on earth, and you wove yourself into them.
You became another shade of thread in the fabric
    of a continent you were born on but did not belong to,
            until then.

Sometimes they mistook their fear for hate.
Men threw their wives' old tomatoes at you,
    laughing late into the night, never forgetting
        the madman who played a flute for his meals,
        or chopped wood like some poor bastard,
        singing his heart out,
        yellow-headed as a canary.
You terrified the men with gentleness
    and made the black-braided women shake their heads.

Once someone threw a knife at you
        (but no, he threw it at the door-frame
        slightly to the left of your shoulder).
Not a single face altered when you gazed up into the crowd.
You continued playing 'Silent Night' –
        a favourite from your repertoire of Christmas carols.
You believe this happened in late July.
But it was a gift, you say, that knife.
Its handle is inlaid with silver.
You still have it.

The colour and heat dazed you, plaited pink
        and black rainbows in your brain at night,
        ribbons of blue, braids of red bandannas.
You dreamed of the burnished black eyes of Indians,
        the green-toothed mouth of the Amazon opening,
                opening, swallowing you whole.
For a time you forgot the sea existed.
You only longed for more of that river's throat.

Slowly, you learned to love the people of those places,
        watched the strong hands of women
        sequined in fish scales and blood,
        listened as men swore at oxen and coaxed the ground green.
They knew the truth but never spoke it, not caring for words.
The sad laughter of the soil was explanation enough.
Brazil's warm contours arched up to meet you,
        mysterious, beautiful as the body
        of a goddess, eyes the colour of honey.

You tell me these stories over glasses of good wine,
        sketching maps on the napkins,
        chuckling for reasons that are beyond me.

You are beyond me.
Even as you eat Camembert, you are still there,
    unreachable, tramping through mud
    on a continent the colour of spring and death,
        two flutes in your pocket,
        a crystal from Argentina round your neck.

When you glide yourself over me,
    that clear stone
    hangs between us.
That small mountain of quartz presses my chest
        before you can,
        carving the distance of dark countries between us.

Journal without dates:
from Paris to Honfleur to Caen

Mannequins chatter on the lovely streets.
The Seine droops waterless, swirling rotten hair.
The Eiffel railway runs a foreign-cattle boxcar
one quarter of the way to heaven.
Hear the tourists bellow delight.
In the Louvre, the delicate Japanese stare
and stare, appalled by Rubens' lolling women.
Outside, in the courtyards, pigeons swoop ominous
as ravens, and dirtier.
The monuments stink of cat piss.
On the streets, we see the frenetic copulation
of the moment on history's soiled bed.

I leave with my hands, catch a ride
from Versailles with the dream of tall trees in my mind.
The first night I sleep in a field and wake up
just before my skin turns to mud and wet leaves.
Grass grows with my eyelashes.
I find mushrooms in my hair.

The next day I walk forever through fields.
My feet cry like pink kittens.
Within ten hours I drop deep
into the loneliness of freedom.
I talk to the grass, the little rocks,
the distant figures of women bending in gardens.
I sleep in the tight shell of my body
anywhere, without dreams, losing memory on the grass
like a snake who writhes away her dead skin.

My lies become historical.
I walk through strawberry fields inventing
elaborate tales of orphanages, seductions, deaths.
The land's memory rises up through me,
turning my brain's black soil.
Sometimes I remember the wars
and wonder if I am stepping

on a dead man's heart, or his hand,
or the shadow of his shattered eye
shrivelled like a grape.
Who died here? I whisper in twilight's ear.
The sky inks out a crimson scroll.

I walk and walk, barefoot sometimes,
the mellow flesh of mud thrusting through my toes.
After a while, I know I amble
through a painting I've seen at D'Orsay.

When I meet the road a century later,
I throw a black stone over my shoulder.
I put out my thumb.
The price of a ride with a stranger
        is words, a little fat,
        a bit of hair, dry paper:
        anything that can be burned.
Remember the body is blooded wood.

Strangers, I say to myself, climbing in.
You are no one but a stranger.
Forget the exhausting habit of tenderness.
I look at the window and instead of my face,
I see his, the reflection of a knife-edged nose
and white-gold hair.
Smile, smile.
I am Danish, he says, I am
going to Normandy, to the sea.
This is romantic enough.
As soon as I close the car door,
everything begins.

*   *   *   *   *

We leave the living behind.
He drives away from those green valleys.
Lives are folded lovely in lace
in little houses, fingering polished forks.
We drive away from the yellow-blue gardens,
children's voices, simple bees.

But I think to myself: be thankful.
I can already smell the deep openness of ocean,
already feel my skeleton sink through water.
The Dane's eyes grow bluer and bluer:
bits of sky snared in a round bone.

The price of a ride with a stranger
is skin, or words.
The man tries to pry me open like a mollusk,
digs through the soft flesh,
searching for my pearl of hurt.
I tell him nothing.

I pretend to forget where I come from.
How did you learn to speak French? he asks.
Have you ever had a lover who died?
Did something bad happen to you in Paris?

I think for a moment of Camille, and tell him,
        I discovered what a beast Rodin really was.
He laughs, he does not realize I am serious.

In the afternoon, he changes tactics, tells me
the sad story of his life, the bitch his wife was.
I am falling asleep, my cheek a pressed rose petal
on the car window. I don't care, I don't care.
He feeds me cheese I can't afford, though
I will pay for it. That's fair.
I can't even afford the toilets in France.

When night comes, he wants a bed.
It is too cold to sleep outside, he says.
The crops grow up around us
like soldiers, tall and ragged.
The corn is starving.
Every hotel is full.
He wants me to go to a farmhouse
and ask for a room in my pathetic adorable French,
but I know the bed would be ancient and creaky.
No, I think, no, I don't want strangers
to hear this stranger
cracking his whip-length against me.
When we pass through the little towns
the silence is terrifying, deep as the well
where the unwanted baby is thrown.

*   *   *   *   *

Finally we find a little inn, finally.

Two in the morning and I'm so sick of him and his probing
intellectual bullshit I could throw up, but he's the one whose
paying, isn't he? I haven't taken a shower or slept in a bed for a
week: I decide to be stoic and pay my dues without a fuss. He sits
on the edge of the double bed smiling with large, very
intimidating teeth, horse's teeth. But it's his blue razor eyes that
cut me up. A true Aryan. I like Latin men, dark men; at least I
know what to expect. This blonde Goliath is suspicious. I can
never guess the motives of the pale-eyed. And he is so big! When
he is sitting, he is almost my height. When he stands, I stare at his
lower rib. He must be six and a half feet tall. I take a towel off the
vanity. 'I'm going to take a shower, okay?' He smiles; I think he is
relieved. I may smell.

In the shower I do not think of him, or what I'll be doing later.
Cleanliness is momentary, like laughter. I let the hot water
convince me that life is a warm kiss all down my body, all through
time. I stay under the hot spray with my eyes closed until I hear a
knock at the door. He even turns the knob. My time is up. I turn

off the water, dry myself, and come out wrapped in a thin cotton towel which has dried over a thousand bodies.

He is not greedy. He doesn't touch me, doesn't leap on my naked shoulders. Perhaps it won't be so bad after all. He takes a quick shower himself and smiles when he comes out and sees that I am already under the covers. He turns off the light and comes to the bed naked. Even in the dark I can see his penis is too big: I am going to be split in half. I am going to bleed. He gets in beside me and puts his head back on the pillow rather stiffly, as if his erection effects his whole body. I am falling asleep, but every time I open my eyes, I see he is staring straight up at the ceiling.

For the first time, I am afraid he is a murderer: in the morning, the hotel staff will discover a dismembered young woman decorating the room. But no. He is just uncomfortable. He has had no cues from me about how to proceed: other women are more encouraging. I don't want to be fucked by him and he knows it, but he also knows that I owe him something. How tiresome. My mind is turning into a soup of dreams: I am talking to him but nothing comes out of my mouth. I see a forest, I am walking towards a forest... Then his hand wakes me up. His hand is on my belly, my hip, moving downward, then hesitating–these things have a proper order. Before he touches my genitals, he must touch my breasts. I smile with my eyes closed and he mistakes my smile for the signal he has been seeking. His touches are the fumblings of a rough and awkward boy. Nothing in me moves. I begin to fall asleep again, enter the trees, the tangle of words and voices from another country. . .

His mouth is on me, my shoulder, breast, suckle, suckle. I wake up again and kiss him with all the passion I can muster, thinking if I don't do something, this groping will go on all night and I'll never get any sleep. I imagine women while I kiss him, the few women, the very beautiful one especially, the one starved for touch. He almost feels like her, if I use my imagination. But he is not so gentle. Suddenly he is on top of me and spreading my legs with his knees. There are two major technical difficulties here: the dryness of my vagina and the size of his penis. It is a cucumber. It is enormous. It takes a long time to convince my sleepy vagina to admit this great vegetable, but after one

particularly hard thrust, he manages to bury himself inside me. I cry out because my cervix has been taken by surprise. 'Not too hard,' I whisper. This is the first thing I have said since I said I was going to take a shower. He thrusts harder. He is an albino bull. I dig my heels into the bed, pushing myself away from him. Harder. His back is a sweating white boulder. Harder. He is whispering what I suppose are Danish obscenities. Harder and harder. I pray that this will not damage me in any way. It hurts now; it really hurts, and I am pressed up against the headboard. I can't get any farther away from him than I already am. He yanks me down the bed again. 'You're hurting me. You're hurting me! Stop it! *Dejame, cabron!*' But he doesn't let up.

I am crying when he finally comes. 'You stupid pig!' I push him off me like a great bloodless side of beef. 'Who taught you to fuck, a mad dog? No wonder your wife left you, you asshole!' I am out of the bed now, I've clicked on a light. My voice is rising. I am becoming Canadian again, possibly even American, because I am so loud. 'You're a fucking rapist!' Blood runs down my leg and I wipe it away on the back of my hand. He sees it and looks down at the crimson smears on his own slimy member. Suddenly he is apologetic, though he continues to say, 'Shhh, shhhh.' I throw a shoe at the headboard, narrowly missing his face. 'You pig!' I slam the bathroom door and twist the water on again. I climb into the hot pelting air, swearing under my breath, crying, furious.

I am not bleeding because he has broken anything, though it feels like he has. I'm menstruating. Perfect timing. I won't tell him that though: he should be left with the guilt of causing injury. Jerk. He *has* caused injury; I stand bow-legged, the way I imagined I would when I was still a virgin. The water whisks the blood and red threads of tissue and sperm away from me. Stupid asshole, I whisper to myself, fingering the raw edges of my vagina, the little tears of skin. Yes, I know, I was asking for something, but I wasn't asking for this. I wince as I dry myself between the legs. I will leave the bastard in the morning, after he buys me breakfast.

*   *   *   *   *

The sea is a dream we crash through
and rise from
shrouded in salt,
the seams of our skin
cracking with dryness.
The sea is a dream if you were born
on the plain, a human pebble tossed
between desert and mountain.
The sea is a dream.

Alone again.
I steal apples, vegetables,
a pair of pants hanging to dry.
A Spanish man buys me beer and cheese,
grateful that I, too, love *tortilla de patata*.
He talks about Spain as if she is the dead woman
he has adored since his youth.
A marmalade cat leads me
through the streets of Honfleur.
I inhale the dough heaven of bakeries.
The children are beautiful here,
green-eyed flowers dancing without the wind.

In another azure town on the ocean,
I cut my feet on the shells
of the elegant beach.
The sky is a grille
of crushed silver spilling gold.
Dusk rolls her glowing body over.
A naked angel slices open the clouds
and crystal spears pierce the water.
I swim laughing through that light,
sea in my mouth, salt in my nose,
my body naked and slick
a seal romping in my skin.
The water is warm, and holds me.

No matter how quickly I move,
no matter how I try to writhe away,
the water holds me, lifts me,
and never once
do the wide turquoise hands
hurt my wondering skin.

But I was born on the edge of a desert
with the bloodshadow of mountains marking me.
I have known forever
the sea is a dream.

*   *   *   *   *

The museum in Caen
breaks the little stick
I have been using for a heart.
Poke, poke.
Even before entering, I touch headstones
and tufts of hair stuck to bones.
A storm of useless blood rises up in me.

The museum stands on a plain of growing light,
acres of grass where the wise never walk.
My journey ends on the cliffs where my feet
founder in the history of wars.
My journey ends at the glass doors
of a modern museum.

I spiral down the steps, stumble
into the black and white hole of photographs.
As if he had been a lover, I recognize Hitler's voice
on the scratchy recordings without reading the signs.
The angular roar and rough snap of German
beats around my head like a scarlet-skinned bat.

Does anyone adore a Fascist?
My skin weeps.
My eyes pucker like mouths
that do not want to swallow
this abundant poison.

The photographs are blown up,
the size of real lives.
People, lovers of silk and silver
candlesticks, lovers of violins, lovers
of chocolate, of air, lovers of
people stagger mute on the walls,
their flesh uttering cries.

Each photograph is acid
poured on the brain's blue rind.
When I have breathed the relic
of this air for long enough,
the photographs grow tongues and speak.
The gypsies, the Jews, the witnesses
of Jehovah, the unionists, the Catholics,
the people, people, people:
each chiselled bone chafes my eyes.
Such thoughtful slaughter.
The fine viciousness of opposable thumbs.
Only those who mourn the murders
they did not commit
remain human.

Who took the photographs?
Did he later leap, flailing,
out of his mind?
Who? These inky tattoos?

The tourists are not sobbing, though
suffering hangs around them like curtains,
opening, opening, falling in red folds,
the drapery of raven smoke.
Even in their cold sleep on narrow bunks,
women wore the stunned accepting faces
of slaughtered deer.

Eyes scarred with darkness
stare at me from cowled blankets of lice.
Scant flesh, but witness the spark
of spirit in those bone-rimmed sockets.
Eyes that startle a camera forever.

I stand before the body of Masha Ruskina
in Minsk, 1941, yesterday afternoon, half an hour ago.
She is slender, seventeen, a partisan Jewess.
Her neck is tooth-marked and bent, a dog's broken stick.
She hangs by her neck in a pale sweater,
blond hair pulled from her face, mouth slightly open.
Soldiers stare at her shins and dangling feet.
I commit her face to my soul.

Beyond me, before the bonfire of bodies,
a child grows exhausted, bored
with these grand visions of murder.
She shrieks like a hungry fledgling
and twists her black hair.
Her eyes are crow-dark.
She wants that green field above us.
She wants to drink and fly
through the sun-hurled air.

Part III: ☀   I Kneel To Kiss The Ice

And only those people for whom their
country is an obstacle rather than an
advantage will have a chance of becoming
truly free spiritually . . .

— *Witold Gombrowicz*

I Kneel To Kiss The Ice

On a day grayer than a bitter sea
I return from the ocean.
My heart red and bitter
    as an ant, so obedient, so familiar,
      dragged by simple time into the habits of blood,
        twitching into and out of shadows,
        twitching to sister-skin,
          my body drawn like an insect
          to this sweet sick dirt.

I return to this country,
    so huge, but nothing grand.
The great trees here entomb me.
Snow angels haunt the air.
The plane burns down the runway
    long silver flame
    trembling.
Trembling, already I am up to my chin
in gravel and poplars, pines,
already surrounded.

The ghosts loom out of the snow
    like fantastic birds
      dancing
      all plume and pierce of talons
      striking, driving into skin,

touching, as lovers touch,
    or warriors in ancient battles,
    the way a murderer grasps weaker flesh

mothers touch their husbands,
who touch their daughters,
in turn, brothers, sisters,
those elaborate battles of small blood,
those memories of a dead dog
and a dead woman who left me
alone in the blue-green world

this white frozen world,
this country
trees, rocks, sky

and streets, the voice of my friend
in her attic of masks and paint:

> this is the city where something
> is always about to happen
> and never does—

streets I stumbled down
laughing, crying, the two words blur,
I dance down the pavement and my feet sting
I had to be born somewhere
I had to be born

the eternal surprise

and I am touched idiotically
by snow, the memory
of my five-year-old soul
believing deeply in diamonds
under the streetlights, blanketing
all the fields, the talcum of seraphs.

I come home
hating this language,
these words, my stories,
my eyes, hands, wishing
only to forget the clamour
inside that has brought me here
again

trolls sleep under
the pink bridge of my tongue

I kiss my mother's cheek
I reach to kiss the sky
Sticky pine sap is on my chin
I have been holding trees
I kiss the door of an old house

I slip down to the creek
on the edge of the city
and kneel to kiss the ice

my lip bleeds a little

I am not surprised.

She Returns To The Farm

Irse es morir un poco.　　　　－Aita
To leave is to die a little.

Volver es una pesadilla. Odio volver.　　　－Noemi
To return is a nightmare. I hate returning.

I come back to an empty field,
　　　gray stones, warm blood beating
　　　through animals that no longer remember
　　　　　the smell of my skin.
And white, scapes of snow so white that my face
　　　is alone with them, my eyes turn to frost,
　　　my jaws stiffen from wind and weeping.

I have forgotten how to speak.
I cannot explain the hands that do not reach,
　　　the feet that walk wordless into the woods.
There is nothing here but fields and freezing steers
　　　and the sharp new teeth of stars.
I find the frost-plumed ribs of an old horse.
The coyotes cackle in the valley.
Even the trees, so keen and naked, are cruel.

Only the snow is not dangerous.
I touch it with my bare hands.
It is violet-skinned and cold.
I want the numbness gnawing my fingers
　　　to mean forgiveness

　　　　but like the skin of a dead lover,
　　　　　the snow feels nothing,
　　　　　　offers no signs.

Animals I Cannot Touch

At night, cows bellow, sway like boats in green harbours.
You rise in the dark to help with the births.
The new calves glisten magical,
    four-legged fish netted in blood.
The animals know the dirt-smell of you.
You walk among the fillies like a two-legged colt.

During the day, your back turns to hard wood
    as you build the stable, turn trees into fences.
Often you bang onto the porch bleeding,
    knee blackened by a hoof, a toe crushed,
        hands puckered with cuts.
Your palms converse hourly with axes.
Pain is seasonal, blazing, like blue sky
        stunned out of storm, it comes,
                goes, mostly it comes but everything
                        grows again.

Your mind a plain gray egg.
When I hear you breathe, I hear wind
    empty of omens, wind artless and warm, blowing
    through the grass-lashed eyes of deer skulls.
Small falcons soar through the canyon hidden in your chest.

You touch me for the first time
    in the library-cave of gleaming antiques.
No one sees us in the elegant old house, hidden
    between the knuckles of mountains.

Desperation is made great by death,
    or dreams, or even by the scent of spruce.
The mahogany tables make me think of aristocrats.
In the library, among books you will never read,
        we crash together,
            two cats
                arching their backs.

Glass eyes—owl, eagle, wolverine—spill a pool
        over prey and stare.
The lynx waits to leap on my shoulders.
Why do I shiver?
Because your mouth grazes my face?
Or because those corpses are so beautiful?

Again, pelts in the dark, teeth tearing
        through breath rising, muscles springing
        against each other, I plunge my hands
                into the silken soil of sex.
Later, when our salted backs lie still,
the crystal eyes of the animals close.

If I write of love, call me a liar.
A pale snail lives in this shell of passion,
        drinking dew, slipping its way,
            a blind eye,
                    through the night.

Mornings, you drink your black coffee
        and walk off, forgetful.
I watch the woods absorb you as willingly
        as they absorb deer.
Even when you stride into the clear fields,
            you disappear.
Animals and earth I cannot touch
            claim you as their own.

This Domain Of Dark Wing

All the clouds come torn to this valley.
They are ragged, refugees
  weeping from their flight over mountains.
They follow the brown, rough-furred flanks of the elk.
Watch their camel jaws chew in time with the green rain.
The thunder reminds their bodies of the spring before,
  and before that, lucid seasons,
  the long hikes of their lives,
  the meadows they have loved in,
  how their mates and children were suddenly cold
    or blood-swept or frozen in the snow.
They lower their heads to the earth
and breathe mist on the worms.

Rain grazes my face
as I haul my cramped heart to the river.
The air sleeps gray over the water.
Everything is its own colour.
New green eyes peer out of the poplar's skin.
The pines have brushed their pointed teeth.
What clean breath these mountains have.

I walk the paths of the forest.
My hands grow cold as I lean over
the deep pools in the river.
The fish there are sentimental,
drifting, their eyes glinting
in the wet-emerald kingdom.

Yesterday
  tons of rock roared down the scree slopes,
  broke out of the mountain's cankered side.
Such noise, a hoopla rumbling down, such an event!
The pika's blood plunged through her suede body.
The gray jays dashed among the trees.
Even the ravens swooped black over the river,
  their wings panting *fear fear* as they flew.

Now huge boulders and stones.
Now rocks embroidered orange with lichen
flood the path.
I clamber over, clumsy goat,
my overcoat sleepy and drenched,
dragging behind me like a tail.

I touch the fallen rocks.
They look like other things,
    long-eared warthogs,
    tiny bison,
    gray dogs barking without teeth.
Some of them are clearly the broken flesh
of the mountain resting on the earth.
For the first time in centuries, rain kisses
their inner skins.

Yesterday the mountain roared,
    part of its body crashing down
    over trees, ants, drowsing butterflies,
    the litter of mice beneath a spruce root.

But that great percussion is hushed now.
I hear the drummer-ghost of rain.
The sky's hand clenches wet cloth.
My boots stumble, awkward on the rocks.
I look at my palms, pink, too soft.
They ask, Is there no other place for us?

The up-ended roots of dead trees
are the time-slaughtered hands
of my grandmother.

Gone now,
all that noise.
Many of the rocks resemble the masks of old men.
There, higher up the slope
 is my father's face,
 his gutted eyes,
 his nose, broken deep at the bridge.

Oh, the rain.
Oh
 is the word the earth whispers
 when we make a hole for our dead.

My face grows wet as I wander
this domain of dark wing, hard hoof.
Yesterday, the mountain heaved for the sky
and ripped open her shoulder.
In the keen wounds of rock, I find
entrails of memory, my own blood,
the petrified bones
of those I failed to love.

Living Nowhere

For T., who committed suicide. The last poem.

Living nowhere now, you are free
to follow me to every room.
You are free to visit me nights and mornings
    and the moment I look skyward for rain
    and see instead the pattern of your scarf
        wrenching the clouds.

No one,
but you weave your veins into a hundred skins.
In strangers' eyes, I see something
    you gave me once,
        a secret, a kiss,
        the unsure strength
        beating in your blue wrist,
        a gold ring from your fist.
        (And even when I lost that ring, years later,
        in an Asian jungle, you were there
        among the shrieks of gibbons, the candied skin
        of snakes snarled round your neck.)

Nothing solid, only a rawboned ghost catching frogs in my mind.
I meet you under the bridge where all the spirits live
    and brown children leaning on the rail
    watch your hands touch my face,
        carve it hollow, stroke it pale.
Is it your long hair dancing on my neck?
Do your fingers whisper in these sheets?
You are the secret spider
spinning in my corners.

You are the shadow I walk into on waking,
    the stain I stumble through each day, clutching
    a hurt I cannot cure, sewing up holes
        in the ruined sweater, the fraying robe, I close,
        reclose memory's broken drawer.
Inside, your photographs grow mythical.

Dear sister, slip away, smoothly, with each year.
Wash down this sharpness, gently flay my fear.

The sculpture of your sere face,
    your choker of collarbones,
    your keen-edged knees,
    these erode.

From an ice-edged bronze
    to a supple heart of clay,
    spin slowly on the wheel of my mind,
        altering, diminishing, turning
        to earth in a kinder way.

The Attic Of Paper Dragons

(on rushing up the stairs to see Christine)

The staircase is crippled now
    but crystals still fire the walls
    and the antique boxes remain,
    trickling rhinestone bracelets.
The book of gnomes and magicians sleeps heavily on the shelf.

I open the door to the room you painted green.
Its floor is still made of mid-summer fern.
Its old desk and cupboards gape open,
    caught in the eternal act
    of an embarrassed goodbye.
The mouths of the drawers are mute.

You left behind what you loved
    but did not need:

    pheasant feathers
    a flag from Bali
    a sheep's skull
    the white jaw of a weasel
      and the old mirror
      stained with India ink

      (but focus past the smear of fingers,
        the scarlet Arab handprint which wards off evil)

       and there is also my time-struck face,
        frozen irrevocably in this room.

Where is the clay, the wood?
Who kidnapped Fetadum and the others, the eerie faces
      leering out of your indigo lands,
            those masks that carved your hands,
                  sculpted your blunt fingers past elegance
                  into tools of Italian bone?

Where are the paint-stained jeans, the orange shirt,
      your life's outrageous rags and hats,
            the road-butchered boots that smelled,
                so gloriously, of horses and sweat?

You took them all.
You walked away wearing those puppets and clothes,
      your own splendid extensions of limb and soul.

This Brighter Prison

I In the photographs, a small boy
     clutches a tattered blanket
     and nurses like a night-eyed calf
     at his own thumb.

These images are now impossible.
Though it is cold,
     the photographs still
     blister my fingers.

The seasons have blurred with the grace
     of blood swirling down the drain
     of a porcelain sink.
Now the boy is rawboned,
     eye-sockets deep as boar-pits.
He leans over the taps and fishes
     fragments of teeth from his mouth,
     smiling at them like curious gems.

Somewhere in this city,
     there are eye-teeth on the sidewalk.
A design like scarlet lace deepens in the snow.
Footprints grate over a glitter of broken glass.
There is a print of a body in darkness.

II I have stumbled over the world's edges,
     licked the candy windows
     and spent endless nights with the wise.
I have watched men and women
     touch each other
     with the tentative
     gestures of stray dogs.
I have seen my happy friends
     tear the nails from their fingers
     and hurl plates out of windows.
I know something about violent bad habits.

But my brother
    who wears the skin of my body
    remains a mystery.
He is splattered by mud.
He is still pelted by orange peels,
    tea towels, and screwdrivers,
        the ammunition of our childhood.

He is fifteen.
He is a gate of anger waiting for the storm
    that will rip him from his hinges
        and heave him to the wind.

III   In the field above Fish Creek
    there are toe prints in the snow,
    evidence of the gallant barefoot sprint
        for freedom.

When he ran, the horses spooked
    like giant gray ghosts and galloped away.
He tore himself through the barbed wire
    and slid down the cliffsides,
    knowing policemen eat too many donuts
        and do not fire to wound.
He dropped his own gun gently, like a black frog.

He ran through the snow,
cut his feet on ice, pine cones, rocks,
sprinting, anxious muscles in love with their bones,
his body oblivious at last, eating new air

    he charged into the trees, bolted
    over the bridge the horses fear

    suddenly he feared nothing

fears nothing, runs,
his mind pierced
with hot wordless sorrow

he sprints out against himself,
escaping into the world,
this brighter prison

the boy, fifteen,
famous for knife scars and theft,
    legendary,
    in his own mind,

      for racing death
      barefoot
      through the snow.

No Green Tongue

El día que me muera / pido mucho sol en el cemetario.   – Marjorie Agosín
For the day I die / I request bright sunlight in the cemetery.

On the first day of spring, nothing sweet
splintered from the earth, no bright birth,
no green tongue, no blossom
wrung from the taut skin of winter.

No. It snowed.
And within my own body
      death lurked like a half-frozen slough in darkness,
      melting, melting, mottled with drowned duck eggs
      and the cracked ribs of canoes.
I thought of the arms of young men severed in warring countries,
      cleaned to a porcelain gleam by ants and maggots.

Marjorie, I do not ask for sunlight in the cemetery.
I want sunlight on the faces of mountains,
      sunlight running down the jade throats of my summer
valleys,
      sunlight on my own face and throat, breasts, fingers,
            through tender curtains of rain,
            through my white cotton skirt,
                on skin, skin.

But long winter coils through me,
a corkscrew of ice and darkness.
My nails tear like papyrus.
It is the first day of spring, now,
a moment named by an idiot in an ugly suit.

How the earth chuckles at our checkered pages of time.
As if the slim poultice of days
could heal the silence seething within us.

Love has nothing to do with closing your eyes

We begin like this:

---

    a needle of breath slipped into the heart
    the sheer line of air down my throat

A hundred minnows are hooked in my belly
by fingers that simply undo my coat.

Nakedness is an old blanket over solitude.
I wait for my legs to stick through the holes.
I wait for moths to land and nibble my eyes.
My hands tell the famous lies.
When I touch, I believe.

When my mind cleaves through my body
and someone hammers there,
fingers wrenching in my hair,
I dream nothing can hurt me.
I dream I am safe.

Later I remember love has nothing to do
with closing your eyes.
My body twists back into itself.
The blanket is yanked off
at the first shudder of day.
My heart is a bunch of dried berries again.
I hear the blackbirds drop down through my veins
to perch on my ribs and peck away.

How many times will this cheap miracle occur?
A shining lake of flesh rises bodily into the air
then evaporates through the door.
All the little fish slap quicksilver on the floor.

An Evening Wake, Its Prayer

What will you do with the cat-gnawed creature,
      the naked shudder in the grass?
You glance up, jaws unhinged by surprise.
Where did it come from?
The trees here have all died.
There are no nests.

Like a peeled fruit come alive,
      it throbs in your palm.
What will you do with it?
You are clumsy, with bear-paw hands.
You might kill it simply by tramping
      across the field, half-leaping, baboon-like.
It nibbles at the fat trap of your fingers.

When you arrive home, it tumbles onto the table.
The blood in your hands surprises you.
Bits of the red jewel dangle from its beak.
It is scarcely a bird.
How easy evolution is:
      featherless and gaping, it is a lizard
      scraped of its scales, bereft of tail.

Ridiculous. Why does everything come to that word?
Tell me, explain the child's game, this absurd gentleness
      with cotton and eyedroppers,
      the white shoebox, the false warmth.
My dear, I will tell you what I've known all along:

      These things always die.

You waste hours, fussing, feeding it.
Expensive meat, too, chopped very fine.
For seven days, slivered screams prick the air,
    fly about the house like needles.
Its neck, I say, would not be harder to crack
    than three toothpicks dropped in a tiny sack.

I tell you to kill it, mercy being its own cruelty.
The raw bird quivers around its skeleton.
Blood sprouts and flowers on the cotton.
Tiny poppies, bitten rose petals, pinched kisses.
Again I urge you to kill it.

My luck, to be with a kind man.
What is the difference, dear,
    between the gentle
    and the weak?

One night I wake, slide out of livid sheets.
I am tired of this dying.
I find the fine braid of bone and nerve
    and knock it over my thumb,
        easy as opening a bottle.
A gristled crack snaps into my own bones.
The bird inhales its death hungrily.
Stillness.

All of this passed quickly in poor light,
    with good reason.
But I do not sleep.
My hands feel like sullen rats.
Outside, I scurry over night's brisk teeth
to dig a hole for this meagre kill.
The grave, one of many, is very shallow,
    very still.
Like the others, it will be easy to open up.

Nothing is forgotten.
Even gentleness fails.
The cotton is never that soft.
You hold a tendril of flesh
in your warm and healing hands, but it still dies.
Nights by all the graves, every one, pass with prayers
wailed to your own cold knees,
your blue-veined thighs,

to the blind dew-worms and their blind god
who is good, they say, and very wise.

Something is burning

For N.H.

I return to the city and find frogs, rainbows underfoot,
King Arthur's steeds on the rocking chair.
Her house is a dripping scatter and spill of children.
They grow so quickly, eyes from gray clouds
to warm blue stars to green stones.
In my absence, they have learned to speak and bite.

Their bodies are small, messed, perfect.
They turn their faces up to me, bare teeth
like fresh rows of corn.
They cry: scraped chins, a comb
twisted in hair, arms caught
in the snare of a sweater.
Then she draws anger out of them
easily, her voice a silver straw.

I arrive and hug her Pablumed shoulders
for just a moment, movement constant,
the kettle shrieking in the kitchen
and the little one waking
in a nest of furious hunger,

and here are the poems by Lorca,
she says, tossing me paper like trick pigeons,
disappearing down the hall

reappearing with Alexander,
a gold brook sliding from the ledge of her hip,
slipping off into a jungle of puppets and dinosaurs.

She is laughing now, stirring tea,
remembering my sugar and not dropping—
       Dammit! she shouts, Something is burning—
anything, not cutting her fingers or crying
but humming among the half-eaten cookies and carrots.
When she finally sits down at the table,
children trot back and forth like small exquisite horses.
She feeds them apples from her hand.

We scald our tongues with tea.
We discuss Byron and the beauty of trees
and the British Museum and the way the world
repaints itself while you lie awake in bed,
listening to the brush strokes in your blood,
breathing the certain silent heat of his skin.
Through the wall, she says, I feel the children dreaming.

Later she drives me home through black nets of rain,
fingers like gnawed leather on the steering wheel.
It's the dishes, she chuckles, I am 68 from the wrists down.

Something is burning.
Even in this wet desert, lives burn.
She takes the light, the clarity of children's tears.
Her hands kindle the clean fire of words.

I lean over the books in my lap to kiss her goodnight,
greet again the sudden blade of cheekbone,
the scent of cold white skin.
I rush through rain to my door
with sparks still on my face.
How she surprises me, this woman
       I have come, stumbling,
              to love.

Words Woven From The Sadness Of Evening Trains

I too have seen faces of dust and grease,
    faces small before hungry cement
    and nameless castles of crystal.
I have seen the mushroom-faced mothers on the trains,
    their children bawling like hooved animals.
They know what they can live without.
They know the aching weight of days.
The women turn uglier with each punishment.
Though they stretch dimes until their fingers bleed,
    an eternity of macaroni lies before them.

The men digging through the station garbage bins
    are resigned to the reek of their bodies.
They have my father's scoured eyes and bones
    chiselled by woodworm.

I have taken the trains of the cities
    and cried in them as a child
    cries in a zoo hung with carcasses.
The wounded people surround me,
    blue-lipped girls roped in cheap dresses,
    boys with ugly mouths, lust caught
    like meat between their teeth.
The people are here.
Their hands are shaped as my hands are.

Even the tears of children are not forgotten,
    their miseries enormous in soft minds,
    dying pets, torn colouring books,
    mysterious torn flesh.
The wail of a yearling speaks for us
    like a shrunken cherub.
Those with teeth say nothing.
We bite our ulcered lips,
    suck on these festering moments
    with mouths that taste of metal and nail polish.

We cough.
Our noses run
    but our eyes are dry lizards.
Beneath their virgin wool, even the businessmen
    shiver in terror from this quick plague of days.
Beyond the windows, our sky unfolds like a black orchid,
    petals infested with glittering mites called stars.

My Photographs Of Madeleine

She liked having her picture taken.
Madeleine had a special way of turning
to the light.
Like finding her asleep on the floor
in a barren room, the photographs
make you want to touch her.
She promised more passionate music
than a gypsy's guitar; even her mouth
was melody in skin.
She wanted someone to play her well.

Her heart was a knuckle of heat
knocking hard at our doors, but we
never opened wide enough.
Smouldering in our own ash days,
we examined the patterns of slush
in the street for portents,
        watched lives from our window sills
        with the concealed savagery of cats.

But our nights were the dreams of dogs:
        quivering, whimpering,
        made of leaps for warm bodies
                that disappeared in daylight.

She pounded for each of us,
        going from one frigid door to another,
        finally seeking the solace of the bathroom,
        the enormous tub with its alligator feet.

Once she yelled down the hall:
        I love this bathroom
        more than I've ever loved any of you.

It was true.
None of us bore the solid heat
of those pipes.

But photographs never show Madeleine yelling.
In the pale graceful face, you meet eyes that dare you to
    screw the picture, drop the camera, come closer.
The dark smile sings you in.

Where are the sticky crimson trails
    she tracked around the house?
        the broken wrists?
In a photograph, no one hears
    screams at midnight, wails,
    curses at Mormons and neighbours,
        the fierce battles she waged
            with lovers, postmen, herself.
She fought with the world at large,
    hated cut flowers, museums, watches.

When they tore down the Mount Royal trees,
    she stalked the city for days
    on a ledge of rage, threatening to leap.

    Nothing is sacred here! Madeleine cried,
    and made love to gentler women in churches.

On paper, she is an elegant animal,
    so still, unblurred,
    not beautiful in the typical way
    but glimmering like a fish
        tossed into the wrong realm.
She had a brightness we turned away from
        as one turns away from too much sun,
        blistered, and bounds for shadow.

But she was not as predictable as sunlight.
The power she implied was storm-like,
    lightning stuns marauding the body.

Only now, in a separate lifetime,
     can I remember Madeleine
     and feel more than an exquisite shudder.
Again, slowly, I am beginning to love her

     photographs.

The Word Is Absurd

Turning away is easy
after a certain arbitrary number
twelve nineteen twenty-seven.
Your lids meet each other, ravaged
flaps of black-stitched skin.
You sleep in a dry well.
You do not wonder about love,
the word is absurd,
no longer taken seriously
by yourself or by any of your friends.
It is archaic, was used by princes
and princesses in stories whose evil witch
always died.
In your stories, the evil witch
gets married.

It's easy, it gets easier.
The darkness in the room
is a weasel curled in your hands,
all muscle, fur, fang.
Through the window, the city spreads out
like a dangerous electric blanket.
Your life hangs black as a bat in the curtains,
drips into the yellow bathtub,
slithers through the intestines of the radiator.

It's not difficult, be practical.
At dawn the sun comes up, the trick works again.

You wake, your face still pressed
to the paunch of sleep.
Outside the ice melts and melts.
The sky is a ripped red sheet.

There is so much to do.
See how far the world stretches back?
It reaches deep into the sky's smooth throat.
No one chokes.
All you do is cough a little.
There are no words to justify lying there,
pretending you are dreamy-eyed.
You get up to clean the sour reek
of sex from your body.

Part IV:　　☀　　A Grand Place, A Greeting

Wherever you are be fearless
And wherever I am I hope to know
You're moving vivid beyond me
So I grow by the strength
Of you fighting for your self,
Many selves, your life, many lives, your people.

– Milton Acorn

A Grand Place, A Greeting

One in the morning, night
a glimmer of streetlights through the glass.
Rain slips out, glides through the grass.
The cool night is wet, a speckled salamander.

I am alone.
This, my skin.
A bruise here, a red scrape, there
    a long blue vein, a river
    on a breathing map.

A grand place, you said, talking of Hungary,
trailing my arteries with your fingers.
Alone, I think of you
    speaking,
    your mouth a chilled caress,
    rain, at night, your lips
      still fingerprinted with spring wind,
      wet on me, this succulent open flower.

Will you slice these petals apart?

I am tired of the little blood,
the yellow smoke of long sadness,
the purple evenings crying in the cave,
    watched over by an imprisoned dog.

If you are lying,
tell me now, I appreciate honest jokes.
I tell them myself,
but those hidden blades hurt me,
the axes and knives in mouths.

I have grown accustomed to blunt objects.
I find it odd that you play the piano.
Don't fool me with your innocent feet,
    lily feet, laughing monkey's feet.

You say they crush nothing
    but leaves, banana peels, over-ripe mangoes.

The scent of wet poplar, rinsed pine
    on your cheek, you whispered,

        Do not be afraid to cry here
        We are extraordinary when we feel.

Your mouth wondered at my neck,
    my thighs, the wet surprised songs
        in this desert body.
And I smiled, dew washed my skin,
        your light tongue rained in

                your body slipped into mine
                quickly, easily,
                a sleek animal greeting earth.

Sleeping Near The Graveyard

We hid in the cold grass
    with death's teeth gnawing around us,
    eating the edge of the city.
Even then we knew the spirits of the dead
    hang green in the trees.
They watched us that night.
Their laughter thrust our bodies together.

Agatha Damaere
d. 1943

You asked, What happens to someone dead
    for fifty years?
Does anyone remember you?

Darkness clutched our ankles.
Tendrils of frost wound up our legs
    as we stood there, trying to remember
      a woman we'd never met,
    hoping we would remember her,
    praying that we, too, in death,
    would be gentled by strangers.

The moon hung above us, bowed in nimbus-lace,
    white hair blown across her face.
She stared down at us like the blind woman
    whose lover never came.
Ember-eyed cats darted among the crypts.

We entered each other quietly that night.
So quietly we whispered and leaned together,
    afraid sorrow would waken
    and knot itself in our hair.

Your blood whirled through your body.
I heard it swirl and twine beneath your skin, burst
        out of your heart again and again, a red
            gazelle, leaping faster, frenzied, flying
                down the tracks of your skeleton,
                    hunted by time.

II Sleep, where we imagine we are safe.
    Sleep, as the candle wades into a pool of blue wax.
    The flame lengthens, quivers.
    You breathe evenly now.
    You swim downwards into the dream-cavern,
        the mad passages of the unroped mind.

    Our skins are flawless now,
            the colour of fawns born
            in blue-shadowed forests.
    You are asleep.
    You are alive.
    I shift carefully, carefully.
    You are the moon's brother, you are a swan asleep,
            too lovely, too distant to watch.

    I can only touch you.
    There, the shadow of my fingers
            a suede spider on the wall,
        and my eyelashes,
            moth wings lighting on your ear.

    As I lie beside you under this quilt of blue moments,
        I feel the shadow of my life
        surge over the shadow of yours,
            slide into the dark socket of your eye,
            lock in the inlets of your neck.

Beyond us, everything—
    the table, the chair,
    the cello tuned with dust—
    ripples with life, our breath, our echoes.
Even the walls and scattered papers pant
    out of the dark
    like wolves loping through moonlight.

Everything grows brilliant in this room
    where you have loved me,
    our bodies falling and opening
    like the jaws of an angel
        learning to sing.

About the author

Karen Connelly has travelled and lived abroad for most of her adult life. Her first book of poetry, *The Small Words In My Body*, won the Pat Lowther Award in 1990. Her second book, *Touch the Dragon*, is a record of her sojourn in northern Thailand. Currently working on fiction and a book about Lesvos, she divides her time between Canada and Greece. For 1993-94, she is writer-in-residence at the University of New Brunswick.

	DATE DUE		
AUG 2 4 1994			
DEC 2 0 1994			
AUG 2 4 1995			
NOV 2 9 1995			